The Self-Determined Learning Model of Instruction

This practical guide introduces the Self-Determined Learning Model of Instruction (SDLMI), an evidence-based practice designed to promote student self-determination and support educators in enabling students to set goals, create action plans to achieve those goals, and self-evaluate their progress. Chapters explore integration with Multi-Tiered Systems of Supports and culturally sustaining implementation of the SDLMI. Hands-on tools for using the SDLMI to support students engaging in academic learning, transition planning, and community-based activities are provided. This guide also features stories from self-advocate SDLMI researchers and teachers highlighting how the SDLMI can be put in practice. Clear and comprehensive, this book is an essential resource for every educator.

Karrie A. Shogren is Ross and Marianna Beach Distinguished Professor of Special Education and Director of the Kansas University Center on Developmental Disabilities at the University of Kansas, USA.

Sheida K. Raley is Assistant Professor and Assistant Research Professor at the Kansas University Center on Developmental Disabilities at the University of Kansas, USA.

T0386189

The Self-Determined Learning Model of Instruction

A Practitioner's Guide to Implementation for Special Education

Karrie A. Shogren and Sheida K. Raley

Routledge
Taylor & Francis Group

NEW YORK AND LONDON

Designed cover image: ©Getty images

First published 2023
by Routledge
605 Third Avenue, New York, NY 10158

and by Routledge
4 Park Square, Milton Park, Abingdon, Oxon, OX14 4RN

Routledge is an imprint of the Taylor & Francis Group, an informa business

ISBN: 9781032102467 (hbk)
ISBN: 9781032080932 (pbk)
ISBN: 9781003214373 (ebk)

DOI: 10.4324/9781003214373

Typeset in Palatino
by Deanta Global Publishing Services, Chennai, India

Contents

1

What is Self-Determination and Why Does it Matter?

Working on my self-determination has opened my eyes that I could do it, but I think I've opened a lot of eyes too …

(Stelios Gragoudas, Self-Determination Researcher and Teacher Educator)

Self-determination is about having opportunities to make or cause things to happen in your life. Self-determined people set and go after goals, navigating around barriers they encounter, accessing the supports they want and need, and advocating for the outcomes they, their families, and their communities value. Self-determination grows and develops as young people with and without disabilities are supported by people they are close to (e.g., friends, family members), by the schools they are educated in, and by their communities to make or cause things to happen in their lives.

(Shogren et al., 2019)

Supporting the growth and development of self-determination in inclusive schools and communities using effective and culturally responsive supports reflects best practice, particularly for students with disabilities as they are navigating the transition to adulthood (Rowe et al., 2021). Additionally, there are commonalities between efforts to promote and enhance self-determination in schools and communities and other approaches to advance social and emotional learning and build executive abilities that are increasingly emphasized in multi-tiered systems of supports (Shogren et al., 2016). But, the focus on supporting self-determination has an important history that centers the experiences of marginalized

DOI: 10.4324/9781003214373-1

groups, including people with disabilities, in defining the supports they want and need to make what they want happen in their lives. The disability rights movement adopted the rallying cry of "Nothing About Us Without Us" to reflect the right and desire of the disability community for self-determination (Charlton, 2000). Disabled leaders pushed for change in special education, particularly during the transition from school to adult roles and responsibilities, to ensure that young people had opportunities to grow in and use their self-determination abilities (Ward, 2005). Other civil rights movements have also focused on the importance of personal and group self-determination, as we'll further discuss in Chapter 6.

Promoting self-determination involves supporting people to grow in their self-determination abilities and skills as well as creating spaces that support equitable and inclusive opportunities to exercise their right to self-determination. Think about the quote that started this chapter. Stel highlights that, to him, self-determination is about learning to self-determine his life, but it also means changing the attitudes of others and creating more spaces that recognize that people with disabilities, particularly those that experience other intersectional identities, have the same rights and opportunities to self-determine their lives.

So, how can we build schools and communities that support self-determination? In this book, we'll talk about how educators and community members can use an instructional model—*The Self-Determined Learning Model of Instruction* (SDLMI; Shogren et al., 2018)—to advance opportunities for self-determination with students with disabilities and their peers without disabilities. The SDLMI enables teachers and other community members to create opportunities for young people to build abilities and skills associated with self-determination (e.g., decision making, goal setting, self-advocating), recognizing that instruction and supports must be culturally responsive, recognize and challenge systemic barriers, and be student- and community-directed.

In Chapter 2, you'll learn about the core components of the SDLMI and its implementation, but first it is important to have a framework for understanding self-determination, particularly how it grows and develops in supportive contexts in young people with and without disabilities.

Causal Agency Theory: The Development of Self-Determination

We've already said that self-determination is about making or causing things to happen in your life, in supportive contexts. So self-determined people are *causal agents*—they act in ways that make things happen. Figure 1.1 highlights three key self-determined actions that support people to act as causal agents: DECIDE, ACT, and BELIEVE (Shogren & Raley, 2022). These are the actions educators and community leaders can support with the SDLMI. Let's learn more about each of them.

DECIDE

Self-determined people act intentionally, deliberately, and purposefully as they work toward goals in their lives. They decide on goals they will pursue based on their and their family and

FIGURE 1.1 The Development of Self-Determination. Copyright 2022 Kansas University Center on Developmental Disabilities

community's interests, preferences, values, desires, and beliefs. They feel empowered to draw on their funds of knowledge to identify and go after the things that matter to them. Self-determined people learn and have opportunities to use choice-making, decision-making, and goal-setting skills throughout multiple areas of their lives, and learn to use these skills together to take steps toward identifying goals for themselves, their families, and their communities. Many young people with disabilities, unfortunately, continue to be denied the supports and opportunities to make decisions about their lives. For young people that experience intersectionality there are more inequities. This is why creating opportunities and meaningful supports across contexts is so important and must leverage culturally responsive practices. In this book, you'll learn more about how to advance culturally sustaining implementation of the SDLMI (Chapter 6) and how to support implementation of the SDLMI in inclusive classrooms (Chapter 7), in transition planning (Chapter 8), and in community and virtual contexts (Chapter 10).

ACT

Self-determined people do more than just deciding on goals that are important to them, their family, and their communities. Self-determined people also take action toward their goals and identify personal and systemic barriers that create obstacles toward their goal attainment. They identify pathways that enable them to navigate around or challenge barriers and routinely evaluate their progress on these pathways. Acting in self-determined ways leads to young people making change in themselves, their schools, and their communities. Opportunities to act are most powerful in supportive contexts that recognize and celebrate the diverse ways that people take action toward their goals. There are an array of key abilities and skills that are involved in acting in self-determined ways, including self-management, planning, self-advocacy, and problem-solving skills. Opportunities and supports to build each of these abilities and skills are critical throughout childhood and into adolescence and adulthood.

BELIEVE

The last self-determined action is BELIEVE. Believing in one's self-determination abilities is shaped by how young people with and without disabilities are supported to use their abilities and opportunities to DECIDE and ACT. Young people seek out supports as they decide on goals, and it is important to ensure that young people are able to lead the process of identifying goals that are meaningful to them and their communities. If this does not occur, young people may not be motivated to take action. And, supportive environments are also essential, if young people feel that their decisions and actions will not be respected, they may also not be motivated to seek out opportunities for self-determined action. Engaging in skills and abilities aligned with DECIDE and ACT is important, but believing that one is supported in their decisions and actions is also important. People grow in their beliefs about their self-determination as they have opportunities to decide and act in supportive contexts that respect their cultural beliefs and values for self-determined actions. This is why Figure 1.1 shows the reciprocal relationships between DECIDE, ACT, and BELIEVE. Making opportunities available throughout childhood, adolescence, and into adulthood and across school and community contexts can support growth in self-determination. People who believe they can act in self-determined ways feel empowered and motivated. They also have awareness of their strengths and needs and of the facilitators and barriers present in their schools and communities. These beliefs empower them to undertake more self-determined actions, challenge barriers, and take steps toward their goals.

Supports and Opportunities

Figure 1.1 also shows the role of supports and opportunities in enabling self-determined actions. All people have the capacity to grow in their abilities to DECIDE, ACT, and BELIEVE, but this growth will be greater when here are effective supports and meaningful opportunities to engage in self-determined actions across contexts. Chapter 4 will highlight ways to assess where young people with and without disabilities are in their self-determination abilities and skills and how educators and community leaders to use this knowledge to create supports and opportunities.

A major support in school and community contexts is the SDLMI, the instructional model that is the focus of this text. Subsequent chapters will talk about how the SDLMI can be used to build opportunities and support for self-determination in schools and communities targeting young people with disabilities, as well as their peers without disabilities. For example, Chapter 5 focuses on how the SDLMI can be used within multi-tiered systems of supports. Chapter 7 focuses on how the SDLMI can be used in inclusive, general education classrooms with students with and without disabilities to set learning goals. Chapter 8 focuses on how to use the SDLMI in transition planning with students with disabilities to engage students in identifying and going after goals for their future. Chapter 10 focuses on how the SDLMI can be used in community and virtual settings to build self-determination abilities and skills outside the school day.

The power of self-determination for impacting the goal attainment and self-determination of *all* students, inclusive of students with and without disabilities, is well established. We will highlight in Chapter 3 some of the key research findings that support using the SDLMI throughout school and community contexts. But, first, reflect on the key values that must drive efforts to promote self-determination, listed below. Also read Stelios Gragoudas's perspective in his *Self-Determination Story* (Figure 1.2). He emphasizes the real impact that self-determination can have in the lives of people with disabilities, and how this has shaped his work educating teachers:

1. Self-determination does not look the same for everyone. The development and expression of self-determination is shaped by a number of factors, including opportunities, supports and cultural values that students, their families, and their communities share. Self-determined people make or cause things

My name is Dr. Stelios Gragoudas and I spend a lot of my time teaching special education teachers how to promote self-determination in their students' lives. I do not think many of my teachers, when I was in K-12, thought that I would go on to get my doctorate and prepare educators like them. Instead, many of them thought, because of my disability, that I should be put in separate environments where I did not have the same opportunities to learn and be a part of my community. If not for my family and my friends, I'm not sure I would have ever had the vision or belief that I could do whatever I wanted to with my life and career, as long as I got the support I needed.

When I was in high school, one of my good friends with a disability told me that having a disability requires planning. This has always stuck with me. A person with a disability cannot just wake up and go to the mall with their friends. They must plan it. They may have to consider things like transportation or what assistance they may need while at the mall. This is even more true for planning for a career, I needed to plan for how to navigate inaccessible higher education environments when I was completing my doctorate. I needed to plan for how to teach courses effectively even when my students might question my competence because of the low expectations for people with disabilities.

This is what made me interested in self-determination for myself, for all students with disabilities, and most importantly for all the teachers that support students with disabilities. Youth with disabilities must learn, practice and master self-determination skills before they leave high school otherwise, they will fall off the transition cliff because they will not be able to plan and advocate for what they need after high school. Too few students with disabilities are able to go on and get doctorates like I did so they can educate future teachers about the real reasons why self-determination and high expectations are so important for all students, but especially for students with disabilities.

I was never taught about self-determination in my public-school education. I first heard the term, when I was hired to develop a self-determination curriculum for students who were transitioning from high school to adulthood. I had to learn fast, but while working on the project I realized that I developed self-determination skills in college. In this environment, I was forced to advocate for the accommodations I needed to succeed academically and find the community living supports that I needed. I also realized my family and friends always pushed me to be whatever I wanted to be and fought against anyone or anything thing that did not have high expectations for me. All students deserve this.

I now train special educators, not only to include self-determination in their curriculum, but to also provide students opportunities to practice these skills so that they can go after the things they want and deserve.

—Dr. Stelios Gragoudas, Self-Determination Researcher and Teacher Educator

FIGURE 1.2 My Self-Determination Story: Why Self-Determination Matters and What Teachers Can Do. Copyright 2022 Kansas University Center on Developmental Disabilities

to happen in their lives, but how they make or cause those things to happen will look different. And, that's something to celebrate! Chapter 6 highlights how culturally sustaining practices can be used to make self-determination instruction more relevant and meaningful for everyone.

2. Self-determination is not the same as doing things independently or alone. Self-determined people have access to and seek out the supports and resources they need to make or cause things to happen in their lives. Some people might need and want a lot of support from others, while some people might need or want less. Some students with disabilities will need specific and individualized supports to enact their self-determination. Chapter 9 highlights ways to create supports and opportunities for young people with complex communication needs. But, always remember everyone can be a causal agent. It is all about creating right set of personalized supports, aligned with student's needs and values.

3. Self-determination is important across the life course and across contexts. Promoting self-determination can and should be embedded throughout education and community life for students with and without disabilities. Students with disabilities might need more personalized supports to develop and express their self-determination, but ultimately self-determination is important for *all* students and tiered supports for self-determination can enable all young people to set and go after goals they, their families, and their communities value, as you will learn more about in Chapter 5.

References

Charlton, J. I. (2000). *Nothing about us without us: Disability oppression and empowerment.* University of California Press.

Rowe, D. A., Mazzotti, V. L., Fowler, C. H., Test, D. W., Mitchell, V. J., Clark, K. A., Holzberg, D., Owens, T. L., Rusher, D., Seaman-Tullis, R. L., Gushanas, C. M., Castle, H., Chang, W.-H., Voggt, A., Kwiatek, S., & Dean, C. (2021). Updating the secondary transition research base: Evidence- and research-based practices in functional skills. *Career Development and Transition for Exceptional Individuals, 44*(1), 28–46. https://doi.org/10.1177/2165143420958674

Shogren, K. A., & Raley, S. K. (2022). *Self-determination and causal agency theory: Integrating research into practice.* Springer.

Shogren, K. A., Raley, S. K., Burke, K. M., & Wehmeyer, M. L. (2018). *The Self-Determined Learning Model of Instruction: Teacher's guide*. Kansas University Center on Developmental Disabilities.

Shogren, K. A., Shaw, L. A., & Raley, S. K. (2019). Convergent validity of the Self-Determination Inventory: Student Report. *Journal of Well-Being Assessment*, *3*, 39–58. https://doi.org/10.1007/s41543-019-00017-w

Shogren, K. A., Wehmeyer, M. L., & Lane, K. L. (2016). Embedding interventions to promote self-determination within multi-tiered systems of supports. *Exceptionality*, *24*(4), 213–224. https://doi.org/10.1080/09362835.2015.1064421

Ward, M. J. (2005). An historical perspective of self-determination in special education: Accomplishments and challenges. *Research and Practice for Persons with Severe Disabilities*, *30*(3), 108–112. https://doi.org/10.2511/rpsd.30.3.108

2

Self-Determined Learning Model of Instruction

The SDLMI provides a way for people to set goals, create action plans to achieve those goals while identifying barriers and solutions, and then self-evaluate progress. The overall point of the SDLMI isn't to achieve every goal (who does?) but to become more self-determined.

(Ben Edwards, self-determination researcher and autistic advocate)

Chapter 1 introduced the importance of self-determination to the disability field, and this chapter describes the Self-Determined Learning Model of Instruction (SDLMI; Shogren et al., 2018) and its core components. The SDLMI is designed to enable trained implementers, including teachers, to support people, including students with and without disabilities, to actively direct their learning by setting and going after goals. When using the SDLMI students learn about solving problems as they take actions to achieve their goals and evaluating their progress and adjusting, as needed. Unlike stand-alone curricula which target specific content (e.g., transition planning, reading or math skills), a model of instruction like the SDLMI was developed to be overlaid on any curricular area. In Section 2, we describe how the SDLMI can be used across school and community contexts to support youth and young adults with and without disabilities work toward goals targeting but not limited

DOI: 10.4324/9781003214373-2

to academic (Chapter 7), transition (Chapter 8), and community participation (Chapter 10).

Chapter 3 summarizes what researchers have found about the impacts of the SDLMI on student outcomes, but for now it is important to know that since its initial introduction to the field (Wehmeyer et al., 2000), research has consistently demonstrated that the SDLMI enables students with and without disabilities to (a) set educationally relevant and personally valued goals, (b) create action plans to achieve those goals, and (c) evaluate progress toward those goals, revising the action plan or goal as necessary (Hagiwara et al., 2017). In the following sections, we describe the three phases of the SDLMI (Phase 1—Set a Goal; Phase 2—Take Action; Phase 3—Adjust Goal or Plan), the three core components of the SDLMI (Student Questions, Teacher Objectives, Educational Supports), and the roles SDLMI implementers (e.g., teachers, related service providers, community members) and students take when they are using the SDLMI.

Three Phases of the SDLMI

The SDLMI includes three phases that trained implementers, including teachers, engage young people in to learn and grow in self-determination. The SDLMI can be implemented each semester in an academic year when used in school settings or over several months in the community. By repeatedly engaging in the SDLMI semester after semester in school or year after year in the community, this provides multiple opportunities for young people to build self-determination abilities as they set and work toward goals. The frequency and duration of SDLMI lessons can vary based upon the context, but SDLMI implementation schedules are typically structured for lessons to occur two to three times a week for a set period of time. This instruction can occur with a whole class, in small groups, or through one-on-one instruction, depending on the setting (e.g., inclusive general education classroom, individualized transition planning instruction, community groups) and students' needs. When teachers and other implementers go through training to facilitate the SDLMI, they learn to customize their implementation schedules to their students' needs, while maintaining fidelity of the implementation of the three core components of the SDLMI (Student Questions, Teacher Objectives, Educational Supports).

In each phase of the SDLMI, there is an overall problem that students are seeking to solve. The Teacher Objectives and Educational Supports guide SDLMI implementers in facilitating instruction to support students to solve that problem. In Phase 1, the SDLMI implementer supports the student to identify and set a goal to solve the problem "What is my goal?" In Phase 2, the SDLMI implementer supports the student to develop an action plan to achieve the goal they set in Phase 1 and identify a self-monitoring process to solve the problem "What is my plan?" In Phase 3, the SDLMI implementer supports the student to evaluate their progress toward the goal they identified in Phase 1 based on the action plan they created in Phase 2. In Phase 3, the student solves the problem "What have I learned?" In doing so, students explore if they want to cycle back to Phase 1 of the SDLMI to set a new goal, if they have attained their current goal, or if they would like to revise their current goal based on what they have learned and create a new action plan. Students may also identify that they want to retain their previously set goal but focus on developing a new action plan in Phase 2 that better supports pro-gress on their goal. As they work through the SDLMI, students learn that the steps (i.e., the Student Questions) are meant to be used cyclically, and that they will work through Phases 1, 2, and 3 repeatedly across semester and years. This creates more oppor-tunities to build self-determination and make progress toward a range of goals.

As shown in Figure 2.1, the three SDLMI phases are aligned with the three self-determined actions introduced in Chapter 1 (DECIDE, ACT, and BELIEVE). For example, in Phase 1, students use abilities, skills, and attitudes associated with DECIDE (e.g., choice making, decision making, goal setting) to identify what they want to learn based on their strengths, interests, prefer-ences, and beliefs and set a measurable, observable, and specific goal. Therefore, if an area for growth for a student is DECIDE, the student and teacher can plan for enhanced opportunities and

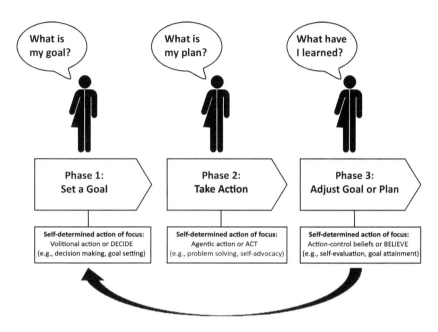

FIGURE 2.1 Self-Determined Learning Model of Instruction Alignment with Self-Determined Actions. Adapted from Shogren et al. (2018). Copyright 2022 Kansas University Center on Developmental Disabilities.

supports as the student progresses through Phase 1. Identified student strengths in DECIDE, ACT, and BELIEVE can and should be leveraged to support the student in working toward their goals using the SDLMI.

SDLMI Core Components

Figure 2.2 highlights the core components in each SDLMI phase: Student Questions, Teacher Objectives, and Educational Supports. With support from a trained SDLMI implementer, students are supported to solve the overall problem of each phase by answering a series of four *Student Questions* per phase (for a total of 12 Student Questions across the three phases) that support them in moving from where they are (i.e., not having their goal-related needs and interests satisfied) to where they want to be (i.e., the goal state of having their needs and interests satisfied). Student

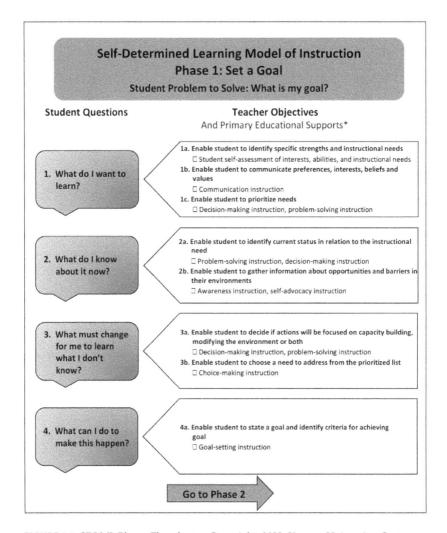

FIGURE 2.2 SDLMI Phase Flowcharts. Copyright 2022 Kansas University Center on Developmental Disabilities

Questions are phrased in first-person point of view (e.g., What do *I* want to learn? What could keep *me* from taking action?) and are meant to be answered by the student, from their perspective. Depending on a student's support needs and their previous experience setting and working toward goals, there is variability in the time it takes students to answer each Student Question. One of the roles of SDLMI implementers is an instructor, and

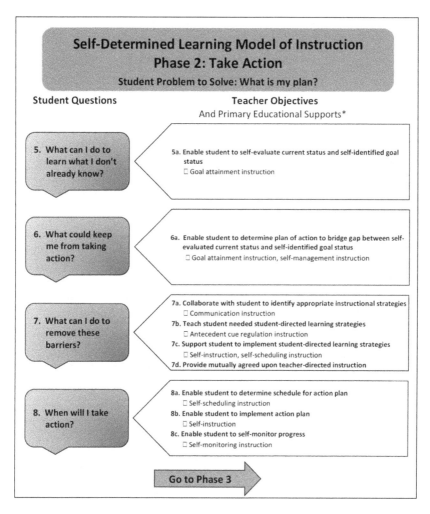

FIGURE 2.2 Continued

teachers must align instruction with each student's needs, supporting them to answer each student question, prior to moving on to the next Student Question. This may involve additional and more intensive Educational Supports. This may also include rephrasing of questions to communicate the intent of the Student Question more clearly, based on student needs. To support all students in understanding and answering the 12 Student Questions, alternative phrasing has been developed that provides additional

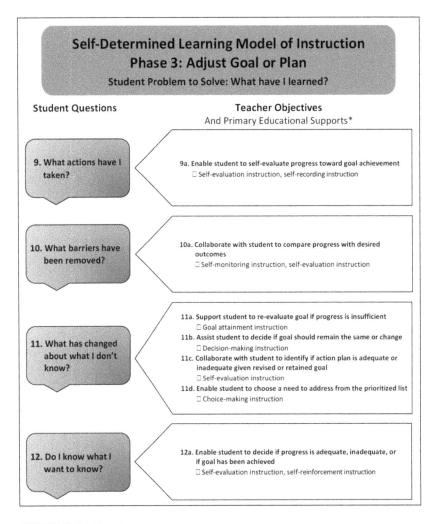

FIGURE 2.2 Continued

ways for students to think about each Student Question (see Figure 2.3).

Each Student Question is associated with *Teacher Objectives* that provide the SDLMI implementer with a "road map" of what they must do to support students in answering the targeted Student Question. For example, to support students in answering Student Question 5 (What can I do to learn what I don't already know?), the associated Teacher Objective (5a) is to enable the

Alternate Phrasing for Student Questions

Phase 1 Student Questions	Alternate Phrasing
1. What do I want to learn?	What do I want to do? What do I want to know about? What goal do I want to work on?
2. What do I know about it now?	What can I tell someone about it?
3. What must change for me to learn what I don't know?	Do I need to change? Should I try to change something else?
4. What can I do to make this happen?	What can I do to make these changes?
Phase 2 Student Questions	**Alternate Phrasing**
5. What can I do to learn what I don't know?	Where do I start? What is the first step?
6. What could keep me from taking action?	What is in my way? What is stopping me?
7. What can I do to remove these barriers?	How can I get these things out of my way? How can I fix the problem? What can I do to remove these problems? How can I fix it?
8. When will I take action?	When do I start? When will I begin?
Phase 3 Student Questions	**Alternate Phrasing**
9. What actions have I taken?	What have I done? What is the result? Is my plan working?
10. What barriers have been removed?	What problem has been removed? What problem have I solved?
11. What has changed about what I don't know?	What have I learned? What progress have I made? What has changed about my situation?
12. Do I know what I want to know?	Did I learn what I wanted to learn? Did I reach my goal?

FIGURE 2.3 Student Question Alternate Phrasing. Copyright 2022 Kansas University Center on Developmental Disabilities

student to self-evaluate their current status and self-identified goal status. Therefore, the Teacher Objectives tell implementers what they need to do to support students in progressing through the SDLMI. Finally, to meet Teacher Objectives, SDLMI implementer utilize *Educational Supports* (e.g., goal-setting instruction, self-management instruction) to enable students to learn the abilities and skills needed to answer the Student Questions and self-direct learning. For example, when implemented in inclusive, general education settings, in Phase 1 (Set a Goal), SDLMI implementers can use the Educational Support of goal-setting instruction to meet Teacher Objective 4a of enabling students to state a goal and identify criteria for achieving the goal (associated with Student Question 4: What can I do to make this happen?). Although there are primary Educational Supports associated with each Teacher Objective (see Figure 2.2), trained SDLMI implementers learn to provide any Educational Support they identify as important to meet the targeted Teacher Objective. As an example, the primary Educational Support identified for Teacher Objective 3b (Enable student to choose a need to address from the prioritized list) is choice-making instruction or supporting the student to select from two or more options based on the student's preferences. In some cases, SDLMI implementers might need to also provide communication instruction depending on the student's communication support needs. For example, the facilitator could support a student to use their preferred communication method (e.g., eye gaze identifying priority area, selecting the priority area using augmentative and alternative communication [AAC]) to select from options. Other strategies for empowering students with complex communication needs are provided in Chapter 9.

SDLMI Student and Implementer Roles

When students and teachers use the SDLMI, they take on diverse roles that are often different from typical student and teacher roles in a classroom. The ultimate goal is that SDLMI teacher implementers and students act in partnership during each stage of the SDLMI when identifying and developing supports and resources for self-determined actions. This can also be a natural time to draw in family members and other community members that are part of a student's system of support. In this way, the SDLMI flips the traditional model of teacher-directed instruction and empowers students to self-direct progress toward their goals with supports they identify. This shows how the SDLMI seeks to advance the disability community's rallying cry of "Nothing About Us Without Us" as highlighted in Chapter 1.

When students first begin using the SDLMI, they learn about their three roles: self-directed learner, active learner, and self-advocate. As a self-directed learner, students self-direct progress toward their goals. It is important to note that self-directing the SDLMI process is not the same as progressing through the three phases independently—we all need supports to make progress toward goals. SDLMI implementers support students to actively engage in the goal setting and attainment process and identify and recruit the supports they need to do so, including supports to navigate around barriers. As such, students are directing the process, but still accessing all the supports they need and want in their lives. As active learners, students act in collaboration with the SDLMI implementer and other members of their support networks. Students become motivated to take an active role in advancing their own learning and navigating through the challenges they encounter. Finally, as self-advocates, students communicate their interests, preferences, beliefs, and values as they set and work toward goals using the SDLMI. Students grow in their abilities to identify needed personal and systemic changes and advocate for those changes.

Teachers who are implementing the SDLMI also take on three distinct SDLMI roles: facilitator, instructor, and advocate. As facilitators, SDLMI implementers do what it takes to enable students to succeed by using the Teacher Objectives and Educational Supports and enabling students to grow and develop in their self-determined actions. Being an SDLMI facilitator does not mean teachers are responsible for making sure every student achieves every goal they set using the SDLMI—we all set and work toward goals that we don't achieve as Ben highlighted in his quote at the beginning of this chapter. Instead, SDLMI implementers provide students with every opportunity to learn from the SDLMI, so they are building self-determination. SDLMI implementers are also instructors in that they deliver instruction that enables students to answer the 12 Student Questions and complete activities identified in the Teacher Objectives. Finally, SDLMI implementers are advocates because they continually support students by advocating for the removal of barriers in the environment and working with students to achieve goals and grow in their beliefs about their self-determination abilities.

With this foundational understanding of the three phases of the SDLMI (Phase 1—Set a Goal; Phase 2—Take Action; Phase 3—Adjust Goal or Plan), the three core components of the SDLMI (Student Questions, Teacher Objectives, and Educational Supports), and the roles SDLMI implementers and students take on when they are using the SDLMI, subsequent chapters will highlight how the SDLMI can be flexibly used across contexts (e.g., transition planning in Chapter 8, in the community in Chapter 10). The core features of the SDLMI described in this chapter (three phases, three core components, and SDLMI implementer and student roles) remain constant to provide a systematic framework to support *all* students in setting and working toward goals they value in their lives.

References

Hagiwara, M., Shogren, K., & Leko, M. (2017). Reviewing research on the Self-Determined Learning Model of Instruction: Mapping the terrain and charting a course to promote adoption and use. *Advances in Neurodevelopmental Disorders*, *1*, 3–13. https://doi.org/10.1007/s41252-017-0007-7

Shogren, K. A., Raley, S. K., Burke, K. M., & Wehmeyer, M. L. (2018). *The Self-Determined Learning Model of Instruction: Teacher's guide.* Kansas University Center on Developmental Disabilities.

Wehmeyer, M. L., Palmer, S. B., Agran, M., Mithaug, D. E., & Martin, J. E. (2000). Promoting causal agency: The Self-Determined Learning Model of Instruction. *Exceptional Children*, *66*(4), 439–453. https://doi.org/10.1177/001440290006600401

3

Research on the Self-Determined Learning Model of Instruction

Teaching is all about giving students learning "handles" so that what they learn is portable and transferable. In my classroom, I want to do things that I know work with students with and without disabilities—especially teaching them skills that they will be able to carry forward into their lives after they leave my classroom. The SDLMI helps me do that!

(Julianne Hunter, early interventionist and transition specialist)

In Chapter 1, you learned about self-determination and its history in the disability and special education fields. In Chapter 2, you learned about an evidence-based practice to support students with and without disabilities to develop self-determination, the Self-Determined Learning Model of Instruction (SDLMI). In Section 2, you'll learn about how you can use the SDLMI to support students *all* students as they work toward academic, transition, and other important goals in their lives. But, before learning how to apply the SDLMI to your teaching, it's important to understand why the SDLMI is a worthwhile investment of your limited instructional time and resources. As Julianne Hunter, a special education teacher, expressed at the start of this chapter, finding "handles" or instructional practices that work and have known benefits for students inside and outside the classroom is critical. There is extensive research suggesting that the SDLMI

DOI: 10.4324/9781003214373-3

does both of these things and that teachers can learn to use it in their day-to-day instruction to benefit *all* students, inclusive of students with and without disabilities (Hagiwara et al., 2017).

The SDLMI was first introduced in the special education literature in the early 2000s. Wehmeyer and colleagues (2000) reported on the findings of a study with 40 high school students with intellectual disability, learning disabilities, and emotional and behavioral disabilities. They found students who were taught using the SDLMI showed greater progress on their educational goals and enhanced self-determination. And, in the last 20 years there have been almost 30 additional studies that have shown the impacts of the SDLMI on students with and without a range of disability labels, in special education and general education contexts, as well as during large group, small group, and one-on-one instruction. The SDLMI has been used to support students to set academic goals (e.g., "I want to improve my English Language Arts grade"), transition goals (e.g., "I want to figure out what college I want to go to after high school"), and social goals (e.g., "I want to learn what sports I can do in my community").

At this point, there is no question that the SDLMI leads to positive student outcomes while students are in school, including enhanced self-determination (Raley et al., 2021; Shogren et al., 2019; Wehmeyer et al., 2012), access to the general education curriculum for students with disabilities (Agran et al., 2001; Kelly & Shogren, 2014; Lee et al., 2008; Shogren et al., 2012), and academic- and transition-related goal attainment (Shogren et al., 2019; Shogren et al., 2012). There is also evidence that when students with disabilities have higher levels of self-determination when they leave high school, they have more positive postschool outcomes, including enhanced employment, community participation, and college enrollment and persistence (Petcu et al., 2017; Shogren & Shaw, 2016; Shogren et al., 2015).

The evidence is so compelling that the SDLMI has been identified as an evidence-based practice that teachers should be using during transition (National Technical Assistance Center on Transition, 2017; Rowe et al., 2021). There is also emerging evidence of the impacts of the SDLMI on outcomes for students with and without disabilities learning in inclusive, general education classrooms where general and special educators work together to support self-determination (Raley et al., 2018, 2020, 2021; Shogren et al., 2021). There is evidence on its implementation with younger students (e.g., Palmer & Wehmeyer, 2003) and in community-based settings (e.g., Shogren et al., 2017). In the following sections, we summarize some of the key research that can inform how teachers use the SDLMI and why this is a strong justification for using the SDLMI to support all students across learning domains. It is critical that information about interventions like the SDLMI is effectively communicated to teachers and teacher's experiences with implementation are communicated back to researchers, creating a reciprocal research to practice and practice to research loop. Only then can teachers and researchers be empowered to make decisions based on understandings of the impact of interventions like the SDLMI on student outcomes. Read about how Julianne Hunter uses information from self-determination research and her own SDLMI training to guide her practice as an educator with students across the life course in her *Self-Determination Story* (Figure 3.1).

Transition Planning

For secondary students with disabilities engaging in transition planning, the SDLMI has been established as an evidence-based practice for enhancing self-determination and postschool outcomes (e.g., competitive employment, community participation; National Technical Assistance Center on Transition, 2017). There have been several large-scale studies that suggest the positive impacts of the SDLMI on transition outcomes for students with intellectual disability, learning disabilities, as well as other disability-related support needs. For example, Wehmeyer and colleagues (2012) worked with 312 high school students with learning disabilities and intellectual disability and their teachers. Half of the students and teachers used the SDLMI and half continued with their typical transition planning instruction in self-contained or resource classrooms. When teachers used the SDLMI, students showed greater growth in their self-determination over two years.

I have supported students as a special education teacher across many life stages. But, a central focus in my supports has been self-determination! And, the research on how to most effectively promote self-determination has always guided me. When I worked as an early intervention specialist, I saw the importance of starting to promote self-determination as early as possible. After I got training and certification in implementing the SDLMI, I possessed the skills and abilities to coach children and their families in learning and applying self-determination strategies across the life course. Teaching toddlers and young children to self-regulate, problem-solve, communicate their wants/needs, and make choices that impacted their daily lives, supported them toward becoming more self-determined over time. This early intervention model, paired with building foundational knowledge of self-determination, strengthens the child's successful transition to school for the very first time.

As a K-12 classroom teacher, I aimed to create a classroom culture where student voice is valued. Providing students with strategies for self-advocacy, choice-making and problem-solving through barriers they experience in society, not only aids students in daily classroom interactions with adults and peers, but also prepares them for the world beyond the classroom. Practicing advocacy and self-determination with my support in a classroom environment where risk taking is encouraged, shifted the focus to a more student-centered approach while simultaneously building the competence and self-efficacy necessary for each student to succeed in the classroom and beyond.

As a transition specialist, my focus has been on aligning students' preferences, strengths, and interests with their long-term goals for education, employment, and community participation. I believe in prioritizing student involvement in all decision making about their lives and future, using research based SDLMI implementation strategies. Often, I find that families and caregivers have engaged in advocacy efforts on their student's behalf for so long, that they need support to shift those responsibilities to their child. If we, as educators, are intentional in our planning efforts and collaboration with families, we can create meaningful ways for students to make decisions about their future in partnership with families and provide valuable input for their own Individualized Education Program (IEP) meetings, short- and long-term goals, transition planning, accommodations and natural supports, and supported decision making, where appropriate. As an educator who is trained in the SDLMI, the SDLMI lessons and the implementation outline are very user-friendly and make it easy for me to deliver lessons to students with fidelity, and plan with them rather than for them, resulting in a profoundly positive impact to their postschool outcomes. This is putting research into practice!

—Julianne Hunter, early interventionist and transition specialist

FIGURE 3.1 My SDLMI Story: Using Self-Determination Research to Guide My Practice. Copyright 2022 Kansas University Center on Developmental Disabilities

And, Shogren and colleagues (2012) found that students with intellectual disability had significantly greater transition goal attainment and students with learning disabilities had significantly greater academic goal attainment, compared to students who continued typical transition planning instruction. And, when students exited high school, if they learned with the SDLMI, they were more likely to be competitively employed and participate in their communities after two years (Shogren et al., 2015).

More recently, Shogren and colleagues have focused on using the SDLMI with students with intellectual disability during one-on-one or small group transition instruction to enhance students' opportunities to set goals and explore competitive, integrated employment after high school (Shogren et al., 2019). A series of studies with 17 school districts and almost 250 students with intellectual disability and their teachers found that teachers can implement the SDLMI with fidelity and that when they do students have better outcomes (Shogren, Burke, et al., 2020). This is true even when teachers combine the SDLMI with other, more intensive transition planning curricula to allow students to learn more about their options during the transition to adult life. Further, when teachers combined the SDLMI with other transition-focused curricula, students with intellectual disability show significantly greater self-determination after two years, compared to students that did not receive the intensive instruction and supports (Shogren, Hicks, et al., 2020). This suggests the power of incorporating the SDLMI into instruction, and the feasibility of doing so with students with intellectual disability, including with students with extensive support needs who need personalized supports to access SDLMI instruction (Shogren et al., 2018).

One important thing that has been learned through the implementation of this research is the importance of high-quality training and ongoing coaching for teachers using the SDLMI (Hagiwara et al., 2020). Teachers require training to effectively implement the SDLMI and benefit from ongoing coaching to navigate challenges that come up in implementation. The importance of coaching has been highlighted by researchers. For example, a line of research has focused on using coaching and other implementation supports to enable general and special educators to implement the SDLMI with students with and without disabilities. For example, in one large project with over 600 students with and without disabilities, students reported greater goal attainment when their teachers received coaching to implement the SDLMI (Shogren, Hicks, et al., 2021).

Inclusive, General Education Classrooms

The first studies of the SDLMI in inclusive, general education secondary classrooms were in math classes. Raley et al. (2018) reported how a general educator and doctoral student, who was a former special educator, implemented the SDLMI with 34 students across two inclusive Algebra I classes over an academic semester (approximately 16 weeks). Students focused on identifying goals related to self-regulating their learning (e.g., advocating for accommodations related to math learning, planning for time and supports for studying and completing assignments). After one semester, over 90% of students achieved expected or higher levels of goal attainment on their self-selected goals. Further, focus group data demonstrated that students felt positively about their progress stating: "I'm proud that I improved" and "It worked because I got my grades up." The participating math general education teacher, decided to continue and expand SDLMI implementation in the following academic year with 81 students with and without disabilities across six math classes, including Algebra II, Pre-calculus, and AP Calculus (Raley et al., 2020). The majority of students receiving the SDLMI showed expected levels of goal attainment, and those that showed higher goal attainment in math-related goals showed greater growth in self-determination.

Larger scale projects are currently targeting inclusive mathematics, science, and English Language Arts classes. Raley et al. (2021) examined the impact of the SDLMI on the self-determination over 992 students with and without disabilities when implemented by 17 general and special educators across six schools and two states in ninth grade core content classes. The outcomes showed a consistent change in overall self-determination for all students during the first year (Raley et al., 2021). Shogren, Hicks, et al. (2021) examined the relation between student and teacher ratings of goal attainment with 647 students with and without disabilities finding that students with and without disabilities could set and rate their own academic goals, and that there was a fair amount of agreement across student and teacher ratings of goal attainment.

However, researchers have also found differences in self-determination outcomes based on students' disability labels as well as students' races/ethnicities. This work highlights that there can be systemic barriers that need to be addressed to promote equitable self-determination outcomes. There need to be high expectations for *all* students, the integration of disability and cultural justice in self-determination instruction, and the use of culturally responsive teaching practices to advance asset-based approaches to goal setting and centering the voices of disabled, racially and ethnically marginalized youth (Shogren, Pace, et al., 2022; Shogren, Scott, et al., 2021).

Community-Based Implementation

An emerging direction in SDLMI research and practice is using the evidence-based SDLMI in the community to enhance school-based supports and services. Although school-based SDLMI implementation has demonstrated positive outcomes for students with disabilities, access to intensive transition planning instruction during the school day may be limited for some youth or may need to be supplemented and connected to family and community resources and supports. Community-based delivery models have potential advantages, including the ability to leverage flexible instructional formats (e.g., whole group, small-group, one-on-one, technology-enabled instruction). Additionally, in community contexts, more explicit focus can be directed to the range of postschool transition goals that are relevant for young adults, bringing in families, community resources, and other learning opportunities. Relatedly, there may be more opportunities to customize the SDLMI to students' strengths, support needs, beliefs, values, and preferences. For example, given the diverse strengths and support needs of the autistic community, we have been working in full partnership with the autistic researchers to supplement the SDLMI to include additional evidence-based supports (i.e., modeling, prompting, self-management, visual supports; Wong et al., 2015) and best practices (i.e., predictable structure, commitment to neurodiversity, focus on high expectations) in autism (Shogren, Mosconi, et al., 2021).

And, examples of successful community-based implementation exist. For example, Shogren et al. (2016) used a modified version of the SDLMI focused on career development for adults in a community-based support organizations for people with disabilities, working with 22 direct employment support providers and 197 adults with developmental disabilities. When the SDLMI was used to guide career development activities, compared to typical practices, people with disabilities showed greater autonomy in their career development process. Dean et al. (2019) used the same approach with a small group of adults and 9 out of 12 adults with developmental disabilities (75%) who had not been previously working in competitive employment found part-time, integrated employment, working an average of 3.8 hours a day, 2.3 days each week.

Additionally, there is a growing push to make sure that the importance of self-determination for young children as well as adolescents and young adults, is recognized as this lays the foundation for the development of self-determination over the life course. Early research established that the SDLMI could be modified and implemented with young children (Palmer & Wehmeyer, 2003) and ongoing work is developing frameworks to both engage early childhood educators and families in promoting self-determination across the life course (Palmer et al., 2013; Shogren, Zimmerman, et al., 2022).

References

Agran, M., Blanchard, C., Wehmeyer, M. L., & Hughes, C. (2001). Teaching students to self-regulate their behavior: The differential effects of student-vs. teacher-delivered reinforcement. *Research in Developmental Disabilities*, *22*(4), 319–332. https://doi.org/10.1016/s0891-4222(01)00075-0

Dean, E. E., Shogren, K. A., Wehmeyer, M. L., Almire, B., & Mellenbruch, R. (2019). Career design and development for adults with intellectual disability: A program evaluation. *Advances in Neurodevelopmental Disorders*, *3*, 111–118. https://doi.org/10.1007/s41252-018-0080-6

Hagiwara, M., Shogren, K., & Leko, M. (2017). Reviewing research on the Self-Determined Learning Model of Instruction: Mapping the terrain and charting a course to promote adoption and use. *Advances in Neurodevelopmental Disorders*, *1*, 3–13. https://doi.org/10.1007/s41252-017-0007-7

Hagiwara, M., Shogren, K. A., Lane, K. L., Raley, S. K., & Smith, S. A. (2020). Development of the Self-Determined Learning Model of Instruction coaching model: Implications for research and practice. *Education and Training in Autism and Developmental Disabilities*, *55*(1), 17–27.

Kelly, J. R., & Shogren, K. A. (2014). The impact of teaching self-determination skills on the on-task and off-task behaviors of students with emotional and behavioral disorders. *Journal of Emotional and Behavioral Disorders*, *22*(1), 27–40. https://doi.org/10.1177/1063426612470515

Lee, S.-H., Wehmeyer, M. L., Palmer, S. B., Soukup, J. H., & Little, T. D. (2008). Self-determination and access to the general education curriculum. *The Journal of Special Education*, *42*(2), 91–107. https://doi.org/10.1177/0022466907312354

National Technical Assistance Center on Transition. (2017). *Evidence-based practices and predictors in secondary transition: What we know and what we still need to know*.

Palmer, S. B., Summers, J. A., Brotherson, M. J., Erwin, E. J., Maude, S. P., Stroup-Rentier, V., Wu, H.-Y., Peck, N. F., Zheng, Y., Weigel, C. J., Chu, S.-Y., McGrath, G. S., & Haines, S. J. (2013). Foundations for self-determination in early childhood: An inclusive model for children with disabilities. *Topics in Early Childhood Special Education*, *33*(1), 38–47. https://doi.org/10.1177/0271121412445288

Palmer, S. B., & Wehmeyer, M. L. (2003). Promoting self-determination in early elementary school: Teaching self-regulated problem-solving and goal-setting skills. *Remedial and Special Education*, *24*(2), 115–126. https://doi.org/10.1177/07419325030240020601

Petcu, S. D., Van Horn, M. L., & Shogren, K. A. (2017). Self-determination and the enrollment in and completion of postsecondary education for students with disabilities. *Career Development and Transition for Exceptional Individuals*, *40*(4), 225–234. https://doi.org/10.1177/2165143416670135

Raley, S. K., Shogren, K. A., & McDonald, A. (2018). Whole-class implementation of the Self-Determined Learning Model of

Instruction in inclusive high school mathematics classes. *Inclusion*, *6*(3), 164–174. https://doi.org/10.1352/2326-6988-6.3.164

Raley, S. K., Shogren, K. A., Rifenbark, G. G., Lane, K. L., & Pace, J. R. (2021). The impact of the Self-Determined Learning Model of Instruction on student self-determination in inclusive, secondary classrooms. *Remedial and Special Education*, *42*(6), 363–373. https://doi.org/10.1177/0741932520984842

Raley, S. K., Shogren, K. A., Rifenbark, G. G., Thomas, K., McDonald, A. F., & Burke, K. M. (2020). Enhancing secondary students' goal attainment and self-determination in general education mathematics classes using the Self-Determined Learning Model of Instruction. *Advances in Neurodevelopmental Disorders*, *4*, 155–167. https://doi.org/10.1007/s41252-020-00152-z

Rowe, D. A., Mazzotti, V. L., Fowler, C. H., Test, D. W., Mitchell, V. J., Clark, K. A., Holzberg, D., Owens, T. L., Rusher, D., Seaman-Tullis, R. L., Gushanas, C. M., Castle, H., Chang, W.-H., Voggt, A., Kwiatek, S., & Dean, C. (2021). Updating the secondary transition research base: Evidence- and research-based practices in functional skills. *Career Development and Transition for Exceptional Individuals*, *44*(1), 28–46. https://doi.org/10.1177/2165143420958674

Shogren, K. A., Burke, K. M., Anderson, M. H., Antosh, A. A., LaPlante, T., & Hicks, T. A. (2020). Examining the relationship between teacher perceptions of implementation of the SDLMI and student self-determination outcomes. *Career Development and Transition for Exceptional Individuals*, *43*(1), 53–63. https://doi.org/10.1177/2165143419887855

Shogren, K. A., Burke, K. M., Anderson, M. H., Antosh, A. A., Wehmeyer, M. L., LaPlante, T., & Shaw, L. A. (2018). Evaluating the differential impact of interventions to promote self-determination and goal attainment for transition-age youth with intellectual disability. *Research and Practice for Persons with Severe Disabilities*, *43*(3), 165–180. https://doi.org/10.1177/1540796918779775

Shogren, K. A., Burke, K. M., Antosh, A. A., Wehmeyer, M. L., LaPlante, T., Shaw, L. A., & Raley, S. K. (2019). Impact of the Self-Determined Learning Model of Instruction on self-determination and goal attainment in adolescents with intellectual disability. *Journal of Disability Policy Studies*, *30*(1), 22–34. https://doi.org/10.1177/1044207318792178

Shogren, K. A., Dean, E., Griffin, C., Steveley, J., Sickles, R., Wehmeyer, M. L., & Palmer, S. B. (2017). Promoting change in employment supports: Impacts of a community-based change model. *Journal of Vocational Rehabilitation*, *47*(1), 19–24. http://doi.org/10.3233/JVR-170880

Shogren, K. A., Gotto IV, G. S., Wehmeyer, M. L., Shaw, L., Seo, H., Palmer, S., Snyder, M. J., & Barton, K. N. (2016). The impact of the Self-Determined Career Development Model on self-determination. *Journal of Vocational Rehabilitation*, *45*(3), 337–350. http://doi.org/10.3233/JVR-160834

Shogren, K. A., Hicks, T. A., Burke, K. M., Antosh, A. A., LaPlante, T., & Anderson, M. H. (2020). Examining the impact of the SDLMI and whose future is it? Over a two-year period with students with intellectual disability. *American Journal on Intellectual and Developmental Disabilities*, *125*(3), 217–229. https://doi.org/10.1352/1944-7558-125.3.217

Shogren, K. A., Hicks, T. A., Raley, S. K., Pace, J. R., Rifenbark, G. G., & Lane, K. L. (2021). Student and teacher perceptions of goal attainment during intervention with the Self-Determined Learning Model of Instruction. *The Journal of Special Education*, *55*(2), 101–112. https://doi.org/10.1177/0022466920950264

Shogren, K. A., Mosconi, M. W., Raley, S. K., Dean, E. E., Edwards, B., Wallisch, A., Boyd, B., & Kiblen, J. C. (2021). Advancing the personalization of assessment and intervention in autistic adolescents and young adults by targeting self-determination and executive processes. *Autism in Adulthood*, *3*(4), 289–299. https://doi.org/10.1089/aut.2021.0010

Shogren, K. A., Pace, J. R., Wittenburg, D. C., Raley, S. K., Hicks, T. A., Rifenbark, G. G., Lane, K. L., & Anderson, M. H. (2022). Self-report and administrative data on disability and IEP status: Examining differences and impacts on intervention outcomes. *Journal of Disability Policy Studies*. https://doi.org/10.1177/10442073221094811

Shogren, K. A., Palmer, S. B., Wehmeyer, M. L., Williams-Diehm, K., & Little, T. D. (2012). Effect of intervention with the Self-Determined Learning Model of Instruction on access and goal attainment. *Remedial and Special Education*, *33*(5), 320–330. https://doi.org/10.1177/0741932511410072

Shogren, K. A., Scott, L. A., Hicks, T. A., Raley, S. K., Hagiwara, M., Pace, J. R., Gerasimova, D., Alsaeed, A., & Kiblen, J. C. (2021). Exploring self-determination outcomes of racially and ethnically marginalized students with disabilities in inclusive, general education classrooms. *Inclusion*, *9*(3), 189–205. https://doi.org/10.1352/2326-6988-9.3.189

Shogren, K. A., & Shaw, L. A. (2016). The role of autonomy, self-realization, and psychological empowerment in predicting outcomes for youth with disabilities. *Remedial and Special Education*, *37*(1), 55–62. https://doi.org/10.1177/0741932515585003

Shogren, K. A., Wehmeyer, M. L., Palmer, S. B., Rifenbark, G. G., & Little, T. D. (2015). Relationships between self-determination and postschool outcomes for youth with disabilities. *The Journal of Special Education*, *48*(4), 256–267. https://doi.org/10.1177/0022466913489733

Shogren, K. A., Zimmerman, K. N., & Toste, J. R. (2022). The potential for developing and supporting self-determination in early childhood and elementary classrooms. In J. McLeskey, F. Spooner, B. Algozzine, & N. L. Waldron (Eds.), *Handbook of effective inclusive elementary schools: Research and practice* (2nd ed.). Routledge.

Wehmeyer, M. L., Palmer, S. B., Agran, M., Mithaug, D. E., & Martin, J. E. (2000). Promoting causal agency: The Self-Determined Learning Model of Instruction. *Exceptional Children*, *66*(4), 439–453. https://doi.org/10.1177/001440290006600401

Wehmeyer, M. L., Shogren, K. A., Palmer, S. B., Williams-Diehm, K., Little, T. D., & Boulton, A. (2012). The impact of the Self-Determined Learning Model of Instruction on student self-determination: A randomized-trial placebo control group study. *Exceptional Children*, *78*(2), 135–153. https://doi.org/10.1177/001440291207800201

Wong, C., Odom, S. L., Hume, K. A., Cox, A. W., Fettig, A., Kucharczyk, S., Brock, M. E., Plavnick, J. B., Fleury, V. P., & Schultz, T. R. (2015). Evidence-based practices for children, youth, and young adults with Autism Spectrum Disorder: A comprehensive review. *Journal of Autism and Developmental Disorders*, *45*(7), 1951–1966. https://doi.org/10.1007/s10803-014-2351-z

4

Using Assessment to Guide SDLMI Implementation

As educators of students with disabilities we must provide our students with the opportunity to build self-determination which will be the anchor to their resilience as they navigate the path to adulthood. Providing students with a tool that facilitates their ability to set goals, map out a path to attain them, and evaluate their role in the process is invaluable for them to believe that they are the causal agent in their lives. The SDLMI is the tool for this work.

(Elise James, Program Specialist, Transition Postschool Outcomes)

Building on Section 1 that introduced self-determination, the SDLMI, and research on the impact of the SDLMI on student outcomes, this chapter describes how to use self-determination assessment to (a) identify instructional needs to personalize self-determination interventions and supports and (b) track the outcomes of self-determination interventions to establish effective practices. We describe the Self-Determination Inventory System (SDIS; Shogren & Wehmeyer, 2017) and how it can be used to identify strengths and areas for growth across three self-determined actions described in Chapter 1 (i.e., DECIDE, ACT, and BELIEVE). Centering students in building self-determination is key and educators using the SDIS can support students to grow in their understandings of their personal self-determination. Educators can also use the SDIS to collaborate with students to share their results with family and friends, identify the way results should

DOI: 10.4324/9781003214373-4

be used in instruction, and emphasize the use of results to drive positive change. This chapter first provides a brief history of self-determination assessment and then describes the assessments within the SDIS (i.e., student, adult, and proxy reports) and how educators can use the results to guide SDLMI implementation.

Brief History of Self-Determination Assessment

In the early 1990s, systematic advocacy for the right to direct their lives by self-advocates with intellectual and developmental disabilities led to federal funding for the development of self-determination assessment tools (Ward, 1988). Two of the assessments that emerged from this work included *The Arc's Self-Determination Scale* (Wehmeyer & Kelchner, 1995) and the *American Institutes for Research (AIR) Self-Determination Scale* (Wolman et al., 1994). *The Arc's Self-Determination Scale* is a self-report assessment with adolescent and adult versions aligned with the functional model of self-determination (Wehmeyer, 1999). The *Arc's Self-Determination Scale* includes 72 items across four subscales: (a) autonomy, (b) self-regulation, (c) psychological empowerment, and (d) self-realization.

The *AIR Self-Determination Scale* focuses on assessing a student's capacities for self-determination and opportunities available in the environment to enable self-determination, integrating reports from students, parents, and teachers. In that sense, it differs from the *Arc's Self-Determination Scale* which is a global measure of self-determination, by specifically focusing on environmental opportunities alongside student capacities. It also includes self (i.e., student) and proxy (i.e., parent, teacher) report versions. The *AIR Self-Determination Scale* includes 30 items across two subscales: capacity (i.e., the student's knowledge, ability, perception to use self-determined actions) and opportunity (i.e., opportunities to engage in self-determined action across home and school environments). Both the *Arc's Self-Determination Scale* and the *AIR Self-Determination Scale* have been extensively used to research self-determination of youth and young adults in context of interventions to promote self-determination (e.g., Carter et al.,

2010; Shogren et al., 2015; Wehmeyer et al., 2013); however, there has been a need for innovation, as these tools were developed in the late 1990s. Specifically, there was a need for tools that (a) are more sensitive to changes in the short-term, (b) are relevant for instructional planning or to inform the intensification of intervention like the SDLMI, (c) are aligned with the most recent reconceptualization of self-determination defined by Causal Agency Theory (see Chapter 1), and (d) integrate technology and the supports it offers for all students. These needs were addressed by a new suite of measures called the Self-Determination Inventory System (SDIS).

Self-Determination Inventory System (SDIS)

The SDIS includes several assessments designed to collect data from youth and young adults (SDI: Student Report [SDI:SR]), adults (SDI: Adult Report [SDI:AR]), and supporters (e.g., parents, family members, teachers; SDI: Parent/Teacher Report [SDI:PTR]). Each assessment included in the SDIS has 21 questions that are rated in a customized, online platform using a slider scale that the computer scores between 0 (Disagree) and 99 (Agree). The custom online system includes embedded accessibility features (e.g., in-text definitions, audio playback). An overall self-determination score as well as scores for the self-determined actions (i.e., DECIDE, ACT, and BELIEVE) are automatically calculated and provided via a user-friendly report at the end of the assessment (see Figure 4.1). After completing a measure within the SDIS, adolescents, adults, or parents/teachers, received the SDI: Report Guide that provides specific recommendations on how people can strengthen self-determined actions across school, home, and community environments. In the sections that follow, we describe each of the SDIS assessments.

Self-Determination Inventory: Student Report (SDI:SR)
The SDI:SR was validated for students with and without disabilities aged 13 to 22 with varying disability labels (i.e., no disability, learning disabilities, intellectual disability, autism, other health

MY SELF-DETERMINATION INVENTORY

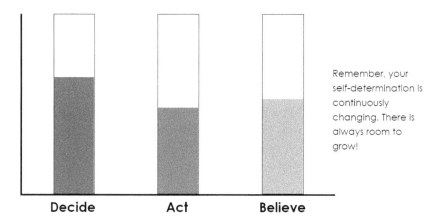

Remember, your self-determination is continuously changing. There is always room to grow!

Decide **Act** **Believe**

FIGURE 4.1 Sample SDI Report Results. Screenshot of SDI Report accessible via www .self-determination.org; copyright 2022 Kansas University Center on Developmental Disabilities

TABLE 4.1 Alignment of DECIDE, ACT, and BELIEVE and SDI:SR Items.

Self-Determined Action	Sample SDI:SR Items
DECIDE	I choose activities I want to do.
	I look for new experiences I think I will like.
ACT	I think of more than one way to solve a problem.
	I think about each of my goals.
BELIEVE	I have what it takes to reach my goals.
	I keep trying even after I get something wrong.
	I know my strengths.

SDI:SR = *Self-Determination Inventory: Student Report.* Reprinted with permission from Shogren et al. (2020).

impairment) and from diverse racial and ethnic backgrounds (i.e., Black/African American, Hispanic/Latinx, White/European American, Other; Shogren et al., 2020), enabling use in school and community settings with adolescents during the transition-to-adulthood period. Table 4.1 provides a sample of SDI:SR items across DECIDE, ACT, and BELIEVE. Research using the SDI:SR has suggested differences in self-reported self-determination shaped by systemic factors (Shogren et al., 2018a). Specifically,

White/European American students without disabilities consistently scored highest on the SDI:SR compared to adolescents from other racial and ethnic backgrounds and with disabilities. Researchers have suggested this results from differential opportunities and supports for self-determination provided by support systems (e.g., schools), particularly a lack of integration of culturally responsive teaching practices (see Chapter 6). This suggests that the SDI:SR can be used to identify disparities in self-determination outcomes and target supports to reduce systemic disparities in education and community contexts. Shogren et al. (2018b) also explored the impact of age and gender on SDI:SR scores, finding no gender differences but expected age-related differences (e.g., younger participants showed lower levels of self-determination). The SDI:SR has also been translated into other languages to enhance language accessibility. Currently, the SDI:SR is available on www.self-determination.org in American English, Spanish, and American Sign Language; however, there are several ongoing translation projects, including French, Japanese, and Chinese (Mandarin).

Ongoing efforts are also underway to determine ways to triangulate data from other supporters (e.g., parents/family members, teachers) to inform instruction and supports. To this end, the SDIS also includes the Self-Determination Inventory: Parent/Teacher Report (SDI:PTR).

Self-Determination Inventory: Parent/Teacher Report (SDI:PTR)

Before describing the SDI:PTR, it is important to note that it was developed to gather information from supporters (e.g., parents, family members, teachers) on their perception of a youth or young adult's self-determination, but it is not intended as a substitute for the SDI:SR and instead should be considered supplemental to a student's own perspective.

The SDI:PTR is comprised of 21 items that mirror those of the SDI:SR. It was designed for use by any proxy respondent who knows the youth or adolescent well. For example, "I have what it takes to reach my goals" is an SDI:SR item and its mirrored item on the SDI:PTR is "This student has what it takes to reach their goals." Like the SDI:SR, the SDI:PTR aligns with Causal Agency

Theory and provides an overall self-determination score as well as scores across DECIDE, ACT, and BELIEVE from the perspective of a teacher, family member, or other proxy familiar with the youth or young adult.

Shogren, Anderson, et al. (2021) compared ratings on the SDI:SR made by adolescents and SDI:PTR made by their teachers. Findings suggested the same questions on the SDI:SR and SDI:PTR can be used to measure self-determination, but that teacher respondents tended to report that adolescents had lower levels of self-determination, although the discrepancy between adolescent self-report and teacher proxy-report varied based on the disability status and race/ethnicity of the student. Discrepancies were greatest for teacher ratings of students from marginalized groups. This highlights the importance of supporting shared understandings of self-determination across students, teachers, family, and community members and the need to focus on cultural humility and advancing culturally sustaining supports for self-determination (see Chapter 6). Future research is needed comparing SDI:PTR results when completed by family members and youth and young adults' reports using the SDI:SR.

Self-Determination Inventory: Adult Report (SDI:AR)

The SDI:AR extends the SDIS suite of assessments into adulthood. The SDI:AR uses the same set of 21 items as SDI:SR; however, changes were made to demographic items at the end of the assessment to capture more information relevant to adult roles and responsibilities, including living arrangement and employment status of adults with and without disabilities. The SDI:AR has been shown to be useful in assessing self-determination of adults with and without intellectual disability ages 18 and over (Shogren, Rifenbark, et al., 2021). Ongoing research has suggested the SDI:AR can also be used to identify disparities and plan for supports that advance equity (i.e., age, gender, and disability label; Hagiwara et al., 2020). For example, adults without disabilities scored higher than adults with disabilities on the SDI:AR, with the largest disparities found for adults with intellectual disability, highlighting the need to challenge systemic barriers and provide effective, individualized supports for self-determination across the life course. This is particularly true because other factors like inclusive education, living arrangement, and employment opportunities also contribute to higher self-determination scores. For example, adults with disabilities who reported that they did not work or worked part-time scored significantly lower on the SDI:AR than those who had full-time employment. These findings highlight the importance of making sure that adults with disabilities have opportunities to engage in inclusive activities of their choosing in the community, consistent with effective transition services and supports planning as youth move from school to adult roles and responsibilities. Overall, the SDIS has significantly advanced self-determination assessment and provides educators with tools to plan interventions and supports for self-determination, including using the SDLMI.

Using the SDIS to Guide SDLMI Implementation

Using results from the SDIS, students, families, and teachers can collaboratively plan for enhancing opportunities and building supports to for self-determination, which could include using evidence-based interventions like the SDLMI. As shown in Figure 2.1, each SDLMI phase aligns with DECIDE, ACT, and BELIEVE so using results from the SDIS can provide teachers with information on self-determination strengths to leverage during their SDLMI facilitation and instruction. For example, when teachers are using the SDLMI, in Phase 1, students use abilities, skills, and attitudes associated with DECIDE (e.g., choice making, decision making, goal setting) to identify what they want to learn based on their strengths, interests, preferences, and beliefs and set a measurable, observable, and specific goal to achieve that goal. Therefore, if the SDI:SR results indicate an area for growth for a student is DECIDE, the student, their family, and their teacher can plan for enhanced opportunities and supports as the student progresses through Phase 1.

Key to effectively using self-determination assessments enabling students to participate and lead in interpreting results and planning for next steps, with needed and valued supports. To this end, after supporting students to take the SDI:SR, teachers can engage students in a discussion about their strengths and areas for growth related to self-determination using the SDI:SR 3-2-1 Snapshot (Figure 4.2). The SDI:SR 3-2-1 Snapshot is designed to support students in interpreting their results from the SDI:SR and identifying next steps they can take to build their abilities, skills, and attitudes associated with self-determination. This is a natural time to talk about what self-determination means to a student and how it is shaped by their cultural identities and values. The SDI:SR 3-2-1 Snapshot includes three sections: (a) students identify *three* actions they can take to improve their self-determination, (b) students identify *two self-determination abilities and skills* they want to make stronger, and (c) students provide *one reflection* they had related to discovering or building their self-determination. Teachers are highly encouraged to modify and make accommodations to the SDI:SR 3-2-1 Snapshot format based on strengths and needs of students. For example, reducing the number of items and calling it the SDI:SR Snapshot can be an accommodation for some students. Other modifications and accommodations include using visuals, enabling audio to text function, supporting students to answer with audio and/or video recordings, and changing the font size and color.

Before identifying three actions students can take to improve their self-determination, students provide their own definitions of DECIDE, ACT, and BELIEVE to share their understandings of these self-determined actions. This is a crucial part of the conversation so that teachers can understand how students perceive their abilities, skills, and attitudes associated with self-determination and the influences of their cultural and linguistic backgrounds. It is highly useful at this stage to engage families, friends, and community leaders in this process, as conversations about cultural identities, funds of knowledge, and how self-determination abilities, skills, and attitudes are expressed in each student's family and community can be enhanced. As students complete this first section of the SDI:SR 3-2-1 Snapshot, teachers can support students in considering what actions they can take to improve their abilities and skills associated with DECIDE, ACT, and BELIEVE before engaging in the SDLMI.

Self-Determined Learning
Model of Instruction

My **SDI:SR** on _____(*date*): **A self-determination 3-2-1 snapshot**

3 What are **3 actions** I can take by _____(*day/date*) **to improve my self-determination**?

DECIDE **What it means to me:**	One **action** I can take to grow:
ACT **What it means to me:**	One **action** I can take to grow:
BELIEVE **What it means to me:**	One **action** I can take to grow:

2 What are **2 self-determination skills** (like decision making, goal setting) **I want to make stronger?**

Skill: _____ **What this skill looks like for me:**	One way I will **grow** in this skill:
Skill: _____ **What this skill looks like for me:**	One way I will **grow** in this skill:

1 What is **one reflection** about discovering and developing your self-determination?

("Ah-ha!" statement, question, celebration, comment, or drawing?)

FIGURE 4.2 SDI:SR 3-2-1 Snapshot. Copyright 2022 Kansas University Center on Developmental Disabilities

References

Carter, E. W., Trainor, A., Owens, L., Sweden, B., & Sun, Y. (2010). Self-determination prospects of youth with high-incidence disabilities: Divergent perspectives and related factors. *Journal of Emotional and Behavioral Disorders*, *18*(2), 67–81. https://doi.org/10.1177/1063426609332605

Hagiwara, M., Shogren, K. A., & Rifenbark, G. G. (2020). Examining the impact of personal factors on scores on the Self-Determination Inventory: Adult Report in adults with disabilities. *Journal of Policy and Practice in Intellectual Disabilities*, *18*(2), 120–130. https://doi.org/10.1111/jppi.12361

Shogren, K. A., Anderson, M. H., Raley, S. K., & Hagiwara, M. (2021). Exploring the relationship between student and teacher/proxy-respondent scores on the Self-Determination Inventory. *Exceptionality*, *29*(1), 47–60. https://doi.org/10.1080/09362835.2020.1729764

Shogren, K. A., Little, T. D., Grandfield, E., Raley, S. K., Wehmeyer, M. L., Lang, K. M., & Shaw, L. A. (2020). The Self-Determination Inventory-Student Report: Confirming the factor structure of a new measure. *Assessment for Effective Intervention*, *45*(2), 110–120. https://doi.org/10.1177/1534508418788168

Shogren, K. A., Rifenbark, G. G., & Hagiwara, M. (2021). Self-determination assessment in adults with and without intellectual disability. *Intellectual and Developmental Disabilities*, *59*(1), 55–69. https://doi.org/10.1352/1934-9556-59.1.55

Shogren, K. A., Shaw, L. A., Raley, S. K., & Wehmeyer, M. L. (2018a). Exploring the effect of disability, race/ethnicity, and socioeconomic status on scores on the Self-Determination Inventory: Student Report. *Exceptional Children*, *85*(1), 10–27. https://doi.org/10.1177/0014402918782150

Shogren, K. A., Shaw, L. A., Raley, S. K., & Wehmeyer, M. L. (2018b). The impact of personal characteristics on scores on the Self-Determination Inventory: Student Report in adolescents with and without disabilities. *Psychology in the Schools*, *55*(9), 1013–1026. https://doi.org/10.1002/pits.22174

Shogren, K. A., & Wehmeyer, M. L. (2017). *Self-Determination Inventory: Student-Report*. Kansas University Center on Developmental Disabilities.

Shogren, K. A., Wehmeyer, M. L., Palmer, S. B., Rifenbark, G. G., & Little, T. D. (2015). Relationships between self-determination and postschool outcomes for youth with disabilities. *Journal of Special Education*, *48*(4), 256–267. https://doi.org/10.1177/0022466913489733

Ward, M. J. (1988). The many facets of self-determination. NICHCY Transition Summary. *National Center for Children and Youth with Disabilities*, *5*, 2–3.

Wehmeyer, M. L. (1999). A functional model of self-determination: Describing development and implementing instruction. *Focus on Autism and Other Developmental Disabilities*, *14*(1), 53–61. https://doi.org/10.1177/108835769901400107

Wehmeyer, M. L., & Kelchner, K. (1995). *The Arc's Self-Determination Scale.* The Arc National Headquarters.

Wehmeyer, M. L., Palmer, S. B., Shogren, K., Williams-Diehm, K., & Soukup, J. H. (2013). Establishing a causal relationship between intervention to promote self-determination and enhanced student self-determination. *The Journal of Special Education*, *46*(4), 195–210. https://doi.org/10.1177/0022466910392377

Wolman, J., Campeau, P., DuBois, P., Mithaug, D., & Stolarski, V. (1994). *AIR Self-Determination Scale and user guide.* American Institute for Research.

5

SDLMI Within Multi-Tiered Systems of Support

SDLMI is for everyone. You can "just get them talking" about their goals, action plans, and self-evaluation strategies!

(Steve Smith, Maryland Coalition for Inclusive Education and SDLMI Coach)

Now that you've learned about the Self-Determined Learning Model of Instruction (SDLMI) and its core components (Chapter 2), research demonstrating its effectiveness (Chapter 3), and how self-determination assessment should be used to guide SDLMI implementation (Chapter 4), it's time to describe how the SDLMI can be used to support *all* students using a tiered support framework. To address the disproportionately poor postschool outcomes for students with disabilities (Winsor et al., 2021), leaders in the field of school reform have advocated for building multitiered systems of supports (MTSS) within schools to address the complexities of implementing whole-school interventions that support *all* students (Sailor, 2008). This reframing shifts the focus to equity-based education (Artiles & Kozleski, 2016), emphasizing the equitable distribution of evidence-based supports and services based on individual student needs. This framework leverages effective practices as well as the strengths and resources that each student and their family bring to their education. Shifting to a tiered support framework necessitates a fundamental shift

DOI: 10.4324/9781003214373-5

in not only how individual classroom instruction and support is delivered by teachers but also requires changes in school systems and structures supported by school leaders. This chapter describes how the SDLMI can be utilized within an MTSS framework to promote access and engagement in self-determination intervention for all students.

Multi-Tiered Systems of Supports

Multi-tiered systems of supports (MTSS) typically include three tiers of support. These include (a) Tier 1 or universal instruction intended for *all* students, (b) Tier 2 or additional targeted instruction for students who need more supports to engage with Tier 1 curriculum, and (c) Tier 3 or the most intensive support which includes additional, more intensive instruction individualized based on students' support needs to engage with Tier 1 and 2 supports (Thurlow et al., 2020). An important feature of MTSS is that the tiers are additive, meaning students who benefit from additional instruction (e.g., Tier 2 or 3 supports) receive this more targeted instruction in addition to receiving universal Tier 1 instruction (Thurlow et al., 2020). In other words, Tier 2 or 3 supports cannot and should not replace Tier 1 instruction. Further, when students receive more intensive instruction, all instruction can and should be embedded within inclusive, general education activities. Tiers of supports should not be equated to educational placement (Sailor, 2008).

Growing evidence supports the positive impact of MTSS when implemented to advance academic and behavioral outcomes (McIntosh & Goodman, 2016). Self-determination leaders have recently explored how MTSS can be used to advance access to self-determination instruction for all students (Shogren et al., 2016). Read Figure 5.1 to learn about Steve Smith's *SDLMI Story*. Steve is a leader in inclusive education and SDLMI Coach and shares how using the SDLMI within an MTSS framework can advance access and outcomes for all students.

To implement evidence-based instruction using the SDLMI within an MTSS framework, it is important to understand how

Over three years, I supported high schools in Delaware and Maryland using the SDLMI as a Tier 1 support to promote self-determination for all students. One of my favorite coaching experiences was supporting a high school general education mathematics teacher using the SDLMI with all of the students in her inclusive class. The teacher, we'll call her Joyce, was unsure where to start—supporting students to set goals, create action plans, and adjust their goals and action plans based on their progress sounded perfect for high school students, but it's a lot! Where do you even start? During SDLMI training, she received a plethora of materials that would support students to engage in the three SDLMI phases, but she needed coaching support to figure out how to use those materials in ways that aligned with her teaching style and the support needs of students.

Our mantra became "just get them talking" and her SDLMI implementation progressed from trying out traditional paper-and-pencil activities to more teacher-to-learner and peer-to-peer conversations. When SDLMI lessons went virtual during the COVID-19 pandemic, these conversations transitioned to online channels and Joyce used breakout groups, Google Classroom, and Google Jamboard to support students to collaborate in real-time. Students told Joyce that this allowed them to make connections with peers that they wouldn't have developed before the pandemic and that they even created real friendships. The variety of universal supports she provided empowered all students, inclusive of students with and without disabilities, to engage in the SDLMI in their preferred ways before, during, and after virtual instruction.

During our SDLMI coaching sessions, Joyce and I looked at students' responses to the 12 Student Questions to determine if her implementation was successful in supporting students to set goals, create action plans, and self-evaluate. We also reflected together on which students needed more support through either small group opportunities or individualized SDLMI Educational Supports. Joyce would provide check-in opportunities for students or engage specific learners who were struggling in answering the Student Questions based on their support needs. Throughout each SDLMI phase, we were able to track student responses and make plans for how we could add more or less support based on their progress.

Joyce was an excellent SDLMI implementer. Her personality and style fostered strong and meaningful connections for her students. She made SDLMI implementation look easy with that personality and also her ability to integrate the SDLMI into the structures of her school and classroom. She infused her teaching style and curriculum into existing structures while she made sure to "just get them talking" about their goals, action plans, and evaluation strategies through a variety of methods. She leveraged responses to the 12 Student Questions to support learners and formed even stronger connections with them through the process. Everyone benefited!

—Steve Smith, Maryland Coalition for Inclusive Education and SDLMI Coach

FIGURE 5.1 My SDLMI Story: Using the SDLMI to Support ALL Students. Copyright 2022 Kansas University Center on Developmental Disabilities

the SDLMI can be embedded in a tiered support framework. Below we highlight how tiers of supports can build on each other to support *all* students to receive high-quality instruction to have equitable opportunities to build abilities and skills associated with self-determination.

Tier 1 SDLMI

When implemented as a universal or Tier 1 support in inclusive contexts, SDLMI implementation is embedded in ongoing instruction (e.g., the general education curriculum) with lessons delivered at the start of a class period for about 15 minutes. While there are constant demands for more instructional time, especially in the general education classroom, using the SDLMI as a Tier 1 support can provide all students with equitable opportunities to engage in and self-direct goal setting for their learning aligned with the curriculum. As further described in detail in Chapter 7, when using the SDLMI as a Tier 1 support with a whole class, implementation usually occurs twice per week, for approximately 15 minutes. During each lesson SDLMI implementers target specific Teacher Objectives and provide Educational Supports aligned with the 12 Student Questions introduced in Chapter 2. For example, a lesson might focus on teachers facilitating instruction aligned with the Teacher Objectives to support students to answer *Student Question 1: What do I want to learn?* SDLMI implementers are trained to link SDLMI instruction to their curriculum and identify ways that students can think about learning and their goals related to the curricular content they are teaching (e.g., mathematics, science, world history). This also provides a natural opportunity to leverage and center the cultural values and funds of knowledge of students and school communities during instruction and promote alignment of student learning goals, funds of knowledge, and the curriculum (see Chapter 6 for additional strategies). By embedding the SDLMI in inclusive, general education classrooms, teachers support students to not only learn self-determination and goal setting and attainment skills, but also to become more engaged in the curriculum, identifying priorities for their learning and linking the curriculum to funds of knowledge and goals for their future. This can increase motivation and student engagement across learning activities.

In implementing the SDLMI, teachers might decide to shorten or extend a particular lesson given students' support needs and other contextual factors (e.g., shortened school day schedule or low attendance or alternatively, high student engagement and more opportunities for student discussion). There also might be some adjustments to this implementation schedule depending on school breaks, testing schedules, etc.; however, engaging students in lessons twice a week keeps goals and action plans at the forefront of their learning (Raley et al., 2018).

When implementing the SDLMI as a Tier 1 support, teachers can select broad goal areas (or "goal buckets") to target through their instruction that are aligned with the needs of their students in the curricular area. For example, teachers might identify important goal buckets related to preparedness for class activities, advocacy skills for needed supports in inclusive classes, or specific content strategies related to the subject area—math, science, English. SDLMI implementers learn to support students to select one goal bucket and develop an individualized learning goal within this goal bucket during SDLMI instructional time. SDLMI implementation enhances teacher's overall academic instruction as students have set goals for their learning, and researchers have found that students are more motivated and take greater ownership with they have a goal related to their learning in the general education curriculum. When implemented in inclusive contexts, students engaging in the SDLMI can also benefit from peer supports (Carter et al., 2005). Students can set group goals as well as routinely check in and support each other on personal SDLMI goals, creating a community and building a culture focused on mutual support and working towards goals that lead to meaningful outcomes.

For students with disabilities engaging in Tier 1 SDLMI, teachers can identify needed accommodations and modifications that enable students to engage with the content. Principles of universal design for learning (UDL; Thurlow et al., 2020) can be integrated in SDLMI instruction. This can benefit all students and centers the needs of students with disabilities. For example, teachers might utilize UDL strategies like using combinations of text, picture-based, and 3D object representations of possible goal buckets (e.g., paper graphic organizers and laptops or tablets representing the goal bucket of note-taking skills), enabling all students to engage in the Phase 1 and selecting a SDLMI goal bucket.

Tier 2 SDLMI

When data from SDLMI instruction and assessments suggests that students need intensified instruction to engage in Tier 1 SDLMI instruction, teachers can provide additional 30- to 45-minute small group instruction as a Tier 2 intervention. During this time, teachers can provide additional Educational Supports based on groups of students' needs. This can provide a time for SDLMI implementers to further break down instruction aligned with the Teacher Objectives, providing additional time and supports for students to answer Student Questions. Opportunities for hands on and exploratory activities linked with the Teacher Objectives can embedded into this instructional time. For example, teachers can support small groups of students by pre-teaching SDLMI terms (e.g., goal, problem, plan, evaluate) to promote greater understanding of key content that is a part of Tier 1 SDLMI implementation and have students identify examples of each of these terms in their lives and throughout the school day. Teachers can also group students based on chosen goal buckets to provide additional, targeted instruction using the SDLMI Educational Supports. Many students benefit from opportunities to further enhance problem solving and self-regulatory skills. For example, during the Tier 1 SDLMI lesson for Student Question 6, students identify barriers they might encounter in school, home, and other environments as they work toward their goals. As a Tier 2 support, teachers can provide more SDLMI Educational Supports focused on problem-solving. Teachers can support students to learn and apply the steps of the problem-solving process, then apply this process by having students brainstorm barriers and possible solutions by seeking out real-world examples from their lives. Teachers can support students to explore how this might link to their learning in their general education class. Other students may need additional supports to build effective self-regulation strategies, such as how to monitor progress toward a goal, exploring different technology tools to track progress on goals set with the SDLMI during Phase 2 and evaluating the impact of this tracking during Phase 3.

Tier 2 instruction can also focus on explicit opportunities for students to generalize what they learn as part of Tier 1 instruction to another content area, like transition planning. Teachers can use the SDLMI Transition Planning materials that you will learn more about in Chapter 8 to support students to begin setting goals for their future, postschool. Teachers can support groups of students to think about postschool goals for ongoing education, employment, and community participation and use the SDLMI Transition Planning materials to structure this process. Teachers can also support students to begin to explore how the general education curriculum and course completion during high school is linked to these future goals, aligning goals across Tier 1 and 2 SDLMI instruction. It can also provide an opportunity for students to begin to engage in career development activities, identifying possible career pathways, learning more about requirements for careers, and exploring career exploration opportunities and internships.

A facilitator for Tier 2 instruction can be a general education teacher, special education teacher, or a related service provider (e.g., guidance counselor, speech and language pathologist, occupational therapist). Tier 2 instruction can also be facilitated by community members or people with lived experience, who have gone through SDLMI implementer training. When designing and delivering small group instruction, SDLMI implementers should collaborate with students to identify and co-create additional examples, strategies, and resources within a classroom, school, home, and community to support students to scaffold their knowledge, abilities, and skills essential to the SDLMI process. This style of individualized support presents the opportunity for the teacher to engage in culturally sustaining instruction, inviting students to contribute to their learning by honoring their background knowledge and lived experiences in and outside school (Gay, 2018; see Chapter 6 for more information of culturally sustainable SDLMI implementation).

Tier 3 SDLMI

At Tier 3, students receive the highest intensity of supports based on identified needs in Tier 1 and 2 SDLMI instruction. Tier 3 supports create more opportunities for students to engage with and apply content learned at Tiers 1 and 2. Tier 3 supports also focus on advancing generalization of learning across tiers and life domains (Thurlow et al., 2020). To support generalization across tiers, interdisciplinary team members (e.g., family members, teachers, school counselors, related service providers, community providers and members) should work in partnership with the student receiving individualized Tier 3 supports to identify when and how the student prefers to receive more intensive Tier 3 SDLMI supports, as well as strategies to support generalization to Tier 1 and 2 SDLMI instruction (e.g., peer supports, technology). Individualizing supports for students at Tier 3 enables all students to more fully engage in the SDLMI linked to the general education curriculum and their postschool goals.

Tier 3 SDLMI supports can provide an opportunity for students who need additional time and support—as identified during Tier 1 or 2 instruction—to apply self-determination abilities more concretely to academic learning or transition planning. Teachers can further break down the Teacher Objectives and provide more intensive instruction using Educational Supports. For example, some students might benefit from additional time to self-assess interests, abilities and needs related to postschool options. Teachers can support students to spend time in the community exploring options. Students can build preferences and identify goals based on this exploration. Similarly, teachers can support students to identify ways that self-determination skills are included in the general education curriculum. By learning about the steps in a problem-solving process, students can learn about how this is also used in science experiments, and devise goals for applying problem solving to science assignments to support engagement in class activities.

At Tier 3, the SDLMI can also be combined with other research-based interventions to intensify instruction. For example, researchers have combined the SDLMI with *Whose Future Is It* (Wehmeyer & Palmer, 2011). *Whose Future Is It* is a research-based transition planning curriculum that uses universal design to engage students with intellectual disability in learning about postschool options and opportunities and how to identify goals for postschool life domains (e.g., employment, community participation) during transition planning. After two years, students with intellectual disability who engaged in both the SDLMI and *Whose Future Is It* showed greater annual gains in self-determination than those participating in the SDLMI only (Burke et al., 2020; Shogren et al., 2020). This highlights that more intensive interventions can be highly beneficial for some students.

Using the SDLMI as part of MTSS can advance learning and motivation across multiple domains, including academic learning and transition planning. This can support *all* students in building self-determination, while centering the needs of students with disabilities and students from other marginalized identities (Shogren et al., 2016). Identifying ways to promote interdisciplinary collaboration (e.g., communication and coordination with Individualized Education Program [IEP] teams about students' SDLMI goals and action plans) as well as strengthening family-school partnerships will enhance the integration of the SDLMI across tiers of support. Continuing to explore the use of MTSS frameworks to organize delivery of the SDLMI as whole-school intervention is critical to systemically breaking down barriers to inclusive education for all students. Considering how to make decisions about when and how to intensify supports for all students to equitably access to the supports they need is an essential part of SDLMI implementation across contexts.

References

Artiles, A. J., & Kozleski, E. B. (2016). Inclusive education's promises and trajectories: Critical notes about future research on a venerable idea. *Education Policy Analysis Archives, 24*(43), 1–29. https://doi.org/10.14507/epaa.24.1919

Burke, K. M., Shogren, K. A., Antosh, A. A., LaPlante, T., & Masterson, L. (2020). Implementing the Self-Determined Learning Model of Instruction with students with significant support needs during transition planning. *Career Development and Transition for Exceptional Individuals, 43*(2), 115–121. https://doi.org/10.1177/2165143419887858

Carter, E. W., Cushing, L. S., Clark, N. M., & Kennedy, C. H. (2005). Effects of peer support interventions on students' access to the general curriculum and social interactions. *Research & Practice for Persons with Severe Disabilities, 30*(1), 15–25. https://doi.org/10.2511/rpsd.30.1.15

Gay, G. (2018). *Culturally responsive teaching: Theory, research, and practice* (3rd ed.). Teachers College Press.

McIntosh, K., & Goodman, S. (2016). *Integrated multi-tiered systems of support: Blending RTI and PBIS*. Guilford Press.

Raley, S. K., Shogren, K. A., & McDonald, A. (2018). How to implement the Self-Determined Learning Model of Instruction in inclusive general education classrooms. *Teaching Exceptional Children, 51*(1), 62–71. https://doi.org/10.1177/0040059918790236

Sailor, W. (2008). Access to the general curriculum: Systems change or tinker some more? *Research & Practice for Persons with Severe Disabilities, 34*(1), 249–257. https://doi.org/10.2511/rpsd.33.4.249

Shogren, K. A., Hicks, T. A., Burke, K. M., Antosh, A. A., LaPlante, T., & Anderson, M. H. (2020). Examining the impact of the SDLMI and whose future is it? Over a two-year period with students with intellectual disability. *American Journal on Intellectual and Developmental Disabilities, 125*(3), 217–229. https://doi.org/10.1352/1944-7558-125.3.217

Shogren, K. A., Wehmeyer, M. L., & Lane, K. L. (2016). Embedding interventions to promote self-determination within multitiered systems of supports. *Exceptionality, 24*(4), 213–224. https://doi.org/10.1080/09362835.2015.1064421

Thurlow, M. L., Ghere, G., Lazarus, S. S., & Liu, K. K. (2020). *MTSS for all: Including students with the most significant cognitive disabilities*. University of Minnesota, National Center on Educational Outcomes/ TIES Center.

Wehmeyer, M. L., & Palmer, S. B. (2011). *Whose future is it?* Attainment Company.

Winsor, J., Timmons, J., Butterworth, J., Migliore, A., Domin, D., Zalewska, A., & Shepard, J. (2021). *StateData: The national report on employment services and outcomes through 2018*. University of Massachusetts Boston, Institute for Community Inclusion.

6

Culturally Sustaining Implementation of the SDLMI

I have a voice to make a choice about my future.
(Ricky Broussard, Peer Leader and Pre-Employment
Transition Services teacher)

In Chapters 1–3, you learned about the history of self-determination in the disability field and an evidence-based approach for promoting self-determination, the Self-Determined Learning Model of Instruction (SDLMI). In Chapter 4, you learned about how growth in self-determination can be assessed using the Self-Determination Inventory System (SDIS), and in Chapter 5, you learned about ways to meet each student's individualized support needs for self-determination through multi-tiered systems of supports (MTSS). Building on this foundation, this chapter dives into another critical issue that must be at the forefront of supporting *all* students with and without disabilities to grow in their self-determination, advancing culturally sustainable implementation of the SDLMI.

Each of us has a unique cultural identity that is shaped by multiple factors. For example, disability shapes a person's cultural identity as do multiple other factors including race and ethnicity; gender identity and expression; language; and family composition and values (Trainor et al., 2008). Cultural identities are "shifting

DOI: 10.4324/9781003214373-6

and dynamic" (Alim & Paris, 2017, p. 7), particularly as young people navigate new and different roles and relationships as they move through secondary education (i.e., middle and high school) and transition into early adulthood. Understanding, respecting, and valuing each person's cultural identity is critical to promote educational outcomes, including efforts to support the growth and development of self-determination for students with and without disabilities (Scott et al., 2021; Shogren, 2011). It is important to acknowledge some students have shared experiences of oppression, exclusion, segregation, and discrepant education and postschool experiences and opportunities. Challenging systemic barriers that lead to these disparities must be part of efforts to advance self-determination and promote equitable outcomes for students with disabilities and for students from other marginalized identities (Annamma et al., 2022).

There has not been enough discussion of how to challenge systemic barriers and infuse culturally responsive teaching practices into self-determination instruction. This has led to school and disability support professionals not having enough access to resources and strategies to implement the SDLMI in culturally sustaining ways, limiting students' opportunities and experiences to build self-determination and failing to center the experiences of marginalized youth. When the SDLMI is not implemented with purposeful consideration and integration of students' and families' shared cultural identities, students and families may feel like goals set using the SDLMI and during IEP and transition planning do not reflect their values, identities, beliefs, and visions for the future. As one mother stated about how she viewed her daughter's goal setting, "when she sets goals, you see a little bit of her cousins, her grandma and grandpa and all of that like a network …" (Shogren, 2012, p. 181). This mother also described how, sometimes, she felt that schools focused too much on independence and excluded family members from decisions especially during transition planning. But, in her large, Hispanic family, interdependence was key to their interactions and what they envisioned for the future for their daughter.

So, how can we make culturally sustaining implementation of the SDLMI a reality? How can we we start from a place of valuing marginalized students and families to ensure *all* students and families are respected and valued during SDLMI implementation using culturally responsive teaching practices? As students move through school and into adult roles and responsibilities, it is essential that everyone have a voice in their lives as Ricky described at the start of this chapter. Essential to this is ensuring that students and SDLMI implementers identify and challenge systemic barriers that limit self-determination for marginalized students. Table 6.1 provides ideas how culturally responsive teaching practices can be used during each of the three phases of the SDLMI (Phase 1—Set a Goal, Phase 2—Take Action, Phase 3—Adjust Goal or Plan). However, these ideas are only a starting point, the specific activities can and should be guided by students, their families, and the communities that support them.

Remember, the SDLMI was designed to be a flexible framework to enable students to identify goals, action plans, and evaluate their progress. As a teacher, one of your roles in implementing the SDLMI is to use effective teaching practices—like culturally responsive teaching practices—that support students to be engaged, motivated, and prepared to answer the Student Questions in each phase. Teachers can and should customize their instruction and supports to the needs of their students and classrooms as they implement the core components of the SDLMI (Student Questions, Teacher Objectives, Educational Supports) that you learned about in Chapter 2. Culturally responsive teaching practices can be integrated throughout SDLMI instruction, and not integrating culturally responsive teaching practices leads to the SDLMI not being implemented as intended and limiting impacts on student outcomes.

For example, when introducing the SDLMI, teachers can support students to think about what self-determination means to them as well as what self-determination means in the cultures that shape their identities. In the introductory lessons of the SDLMI (i.e., Preliminary Conversations when teachers introduce self-determination and the SDLMI), SDLMI implementers can use a wide array of resources to infuse greater discussion of disability history, including the disability rights movement, into the curriculum for all students, raising awareness of disability

TABLE 6.1 Aligning Culturally Responsive Teaching Practices with the SDLMI Phases.

SDLMI Phase	Culturally Responsive Teaching Practices
Preliminary Conversations	• Use a variety of resources (e.g., books, articles, films, music, podcasts) to share how people define self-determination from various cultural perspectives. • Invite guest speakers from the community, who share cultural identities and experiences with students, to talk about what self-determination means to them. • Offer options for students to share and collaborate to define self-determination with their peers.
Phase 1: Set a Goal	• Support students to identify their values and preferences for decision making and goal setting—encourage them to ask their families and their friends for their perspective and integrate their values into their SDLMI Student Question responses. • Plan for community-based experiences and connections with people who share cultural identities and experiences to enable students to collectively learn about goal setting. • Seek out and support students to explore systemic barriers they encounter as they work to identify goals—focus on how advocacy and social justice can remove barriers and create more opportunities for self-determination. • Support students to activate their past experiences and learning as they answer the 12 Student Questions.
Phase 2: Take Action	• Enable students to explore community resources, including resources in the local community that can support them to carry out their action plans. • Identify advocacy opportunities, when there are systemic barriers to students implementing action plans. • Assist students to identify ways that they have taken action in the past, then design or co-design self-monitoring tools based on prior knowledge and experiences. • Embed collaborative learning opportunities to enable students to work with peers and community mentors to challenge systemic barriers to remove barriers and advance equity.
Phase 3: Adjust Goal or Plan	• Support student self-reflection on their progress on their goals. Create opportunities for them to get their family and friends input, especially as they are deciding how they want to adjust their goal or action plan. • Have students reflect on what they did in the past when they met or needed to revise a goal. • Find a time for celebration—invite friends, family, and community members to come together to celebrate progress on goals. Have students identify different cultural traditions that can be embedded into an evening or community event.

culture and advancing a focus on social justice. Disabled leaders, alongside other marginalized groups, have sought out recognition that they share a unique history, community values, and the right to be involved in decisions about their lives. This movement is broadening the lens of how society defines "normal" and creates more opportunities for diversity and equity in self-determination opportunities. Supporting students in understanding these movements can support them to vision their roles in advocacy and in goal setting and action planning. Read how Ricky Broussard, whose quote started this chapter, supports adolescents with multiple cultural identities to grow in their self-determination and self-advocacy by acting as a Peer Leader and Pre-Employment Transition Services teacher in his *Self-Determination Story*, Figure 6.1. Integrating students' cultural identities early in SDLMI implementation communicates to students that their cultural identities as well as their individual preferences, interests, beliefs, and values are a priority in context of the SDLMI, building trust and respect as teachers and students taken on SDLMI roles as described in Chapter 2.

Students can also benefit from learning how self-determination is defined in other cultures, and how it has been used to advance social justice. For example, the Indian Self-Determination and Education Assistance Act, first passed in 1975, focuses on the right of Native Peoples to have ownership over programs and services that impacted their lives. The second principle of Kwanza, a celebration of African and African American culture, is Kujichagulia, or self-determination, which celebrates defining, naming, and creating spaces to speak for oneself and one's community. Collective self-determination focuses on advancing cultural justice. By raising your awareness as a teacher and ensuring that students are exposed to perspectives representing the range of cultural experiences and identities that are present in our society, we can advance equity and break down systemic barriers and biases. Essential to advancing self-determination and cultural justice is acknowledging the importance of personal growth and development as well as the need for systemic change.

I love working with students. As a Peer Leader at Imagine Enterprises and a Pre-Employment Transition Services teacher I get to go into high school classrooms to work with students with disabilities 1-2 days a week. We talk about their future and the goals they want to achieve, particularly as they think about transitioning to adult life. My mission is to support *all* students with disabilities to have a voice and learn the advocacy skills they need to go after their goals. I've learned this has to align with who students are and how they and their family and friends think about their goals and their dreams.

Self-determination and advocacy has been essential to my life. When I was 10, I had to leave my home because it was not accessible, and then I had to live in different institutions for a number of years. In these places, I never had real career opportunities, because other people did not support my dreams and plans for my future. I worried I would never be able to get a real job because the people around me did not believe in me. But, when I found Imagine Enterprises and my circle of support, I found a different path forward. I want all students to never have the worries I did. I want them to have circles of support and for their right to transition services be respected and honored. In Texas, where I live, I advocated for the Ricky Broussard Act to make sure that transition services are available to all high schoolers, regardless of where they live or their cultural identities.

I believe it is so important to give each student a voice, and to not let expectations drop for students just because of who they are. I've supported students in the classes I teach, from many different cultural backgrounds, who speak many different languages, and who have many different goals and visions for the future. It is important to celebrate those backgrounds and learn how disability rights advocates have created more opportunities for all of us. I use my lived experiences to connect with students and talk about what is possible—and show them how using my voice has let me advocate and have my dream job and how they can do that too.

For teachers who are using the SDLMI and supporting students to find their voice, I encourage you to always think about:

1. **Using Peer Mentors and Leaders**—people with disability have the right to connect to each other and learn from each other's experiences; there is a shared disability culture and this must be part of the curriculum; and people with disabilities like me should have jobs as teachers and supporters!

2. **Building Circles of Supports**—identify people including family, friends, disability support providers, community members that can brainstorm and help implement young people's action plans for their goals. But, also remember sometimes teachers and others need to "step back and support"—let the young person drive the process, but be there for them.

3. **Supporting Young People to Find their Voice**—everyone has a voice, some people just need more support to have ways to use their voice. Remember that people can communicate and have a voice in their lives in multiple ways, some people talk, others use pictures, others might use their computers—find what works for everyone.

4. **Identifying Roles and Opportunities**—we all want to do things that matter. Make sure the content that you are teaching matters to the lives of each student and their backgrounds and goals. Make sure that everyone feels engaged and connected. People need to have a role in defining their future and their learning—otherwise they won't want to take action.

5. **Having a Sense of Humor**—transition isn't easy. Think about how a sense of humor can be an effective tool in many situations to navigate around barriers, build social relationships, and recognize the absurdity of some of the policies and practices that are still on the books.

6. **Teaching Content, Building Vocabulary, Celebrating Advocacy**—focus on teaching words and phrases, and using tools like the SDLMI that young people can take with them into other parts of their lives—goals and advocacy are important everywhere! The mantra at the start of this chapter is something I use a lot. And, make sure to celebrate advocacy. When young people find their voice, they will ask for what they want and need. Respect them as they do this!

—Ricky Broussard, Peer Leader and Pre-Employment Transition Services teacher

FIGURE 6.1 My Self-Determination Story: Ricky Broussard. Copyright 2022 Kansas University Center on Developmental Disabilities; photo courtesy of Imagine Enterprises

This dual focus on personal growth and systems change can be brought into SDLMI instruction. For example, during Phase 1: Set a Goal, students might focus on personal goals related to their learning and postschool plans (e.g., attending college), but they can also focus on goals that tackle systemic changes needed to ensure that all young people's community, history, and culture and values are recognized and celebrated. During Phase 2: Take Action, as students are action planning, there is an explicit focus on identifying barriers to making progress toward one's goal. Students may identify systemic barriers that limit their progress toward their goals and can brainstorm with their teachers, peers, families, and other community members on ways to tackle issues related to systemic bias. Educational Supports can be used to support students to problem solve how to navigate and challenge structural inequities, address explicit and implicit bias, as well as advocate for individual and communal rights and high expectations for themselves and others, leading to improved outcomes (Aceves & Orosco, 2014; Hsieh et al., 2021).

During Phase 3: Adjust Goal or Plan, students can consider ways that they want to evaluate progress on their goals, thinking about how they might want to engage their families and friends, and what changes they might want to make to their goal setting and action planning process based on what they have learned about themselves. Exploring how the SDLMI can be more culturally sustaining can be a part of ongoing discussions with students, particularly to explore additional, culturally responsive supports that can be embedded in each of the SDLMI phases. Celebrating with students, families, and communities can be a great way to build community and share progress and impacts of the SDLMI.

Overall, to engage in culturally sustaining SDLMI implementation, there must be a strong focus on the strengths marginalized youth with disabilities bring to self-determination instruction, their schools, and their communities. Self-determination is a key part of many cultural identities and discussing different ways that self-determination is understood can be a key part of self-determination instruction, as well as the overall school curriculum. Culturally responsive teaching practices can advance equity and challenge systemic barriers, and should always be a part of teaching, including during self-determination and SDLMI instruction.

References

Aceves, T. C., & Orosco, M. J. (2014). *Culturally responsive teaching* (Document No. IC-2). Collaboration for Effective Educator, Development, Accountability, and Reform Center. http://ceedar.education.ufl.edu/tools/innovation-configurations/

Alim, H. S., & Paris, D. (2017). What is culturally sustaining pedagogy and why does it matter? In D. Paris & H. S. Alim (Eds.), *Culturally sustaining pedagogies: Teaching and learning for justice in a changing world* (pp. 1–24). Teachers College Press.

Annamma, S. A., Ferri, B. A., & Connor, D. J. (Eds.). (2022). *DisCrit expanded: Reverberations, ruptures, and inquiries.* Teachers College Press.

Hsieh, B., Achola, E. O., Reese, L., Keirn, T., Davis, S., Navarro, O., & Moreno, J. F. (2021). Transforming educator practice through a culturally responsive and sustaining pedagogies rubric: Co-construction, implementation, and reflection. In E. Cain, R. Filback, & J. Crawford (Eds.), *Cases on academic program redesign for greater racial and social justice* (pp. 191–211). IGI Global.

Scott, L. A., Thoma, C. A., Gokita, T., Bruno, L., Ruiz, A. B., Brendli, K., Taylor, J., & Vitullo, V. (2021). I'm trying to make myself happy: Black students with IDD and families on promoting self-determination during transition. *Inclusion, 9*(3), 170–188. https://doi.org/10.1352/2326-6988-9.3.170

Shogren, K. A. (2011). Culture and self-determination: A synthesis of the literature and directions for future research and practice. *Career Development for Exceptional Individuals, 34*(2), 115–127. https://doi.org/10.1177/0885728811398271

Shogren, K. A. (2012). Hispanic mothers' perceptions of self-determination. *Research and Practice for Persons with Severe Disabilities, 37*(3), 170–184. https://doi.org/10.2511/027494812804153561

Trainor, A. A., Lindstrom, L., Simon-Burroughs, M., Martin, J. E., & Sorrells, A. M. (2008). From marginalized to maximized opportunities for diverse youths with disabilities: A position paper of the division on career development and transition. *Career Development for Exceptional Individuals, 31*(1), 56–64. https://doi.org/10.1177/0885728807313777

7
Inclusive Contexts and the SDLMI

> Simply providing students opportunities and experiences to set their own goals
> and work toward achieving them was the key to getting to know and support them
> as they progress through high school. Self-determination was making a difference
> for ALL my students!
>
> (Annette McDonald, high school mathematics
> teacher and SDLMI coach)

The SDLMI can be used in inclusive, general education classrooms to support all students, including students with and without disabilities, to build self-determination abilities and work
toward goals focused on academic learning (e.g., Raley et al.,
2021; Shogren et al., 2021). College and career readiness frameworks consistently identify abilities and skills associated with
self-determination as critical for all students' postschool success
(Lombardi et al., 2018; Rowe et al., 2021). And promoting self-
determination can center the experiences of students with disabilities in inclusive classrooms (Ward, 2005). As highlighted by
Annette McDonald in the quote that started this chapter and in
her *My SDLMI Story* (Figure 7.1), self-determination is important
for everyone, and all students should have opportunities and
experiences to build self-determination in inclusive contexts. To
this end, leaders in school reform have advocated for conceptu-
alizing instruction to build self-determination within a multi-
tiered systems of support framework (see Chapter 5) to provide
opportunities and experiences for all students to set and go after

DOI: 10.4324/9781003214373-7

Over 30 years of teaching mathematics has taught me that every student has limitless potential and as a teacher, I look for strategies to support students identifying their strengths and work toward goals they find meaningful in their lives. For my high school students, long-term goals often include getting accepted into their dream college, securing an internship at a company they admire, or for some students, simply graduating with their friends.

Using the SDLMI provided me with an evidence-based practice I can use to support my students in taking their long-term goals and identifying how they can set related short-term goals. Students work toward their goal using the SDLMI during the semester to bring them one step closer to their long-term goal. For example, my Algebra I ninth graders are notorious for being late to class or missing it all together, so when we talk about their long-term goal to graduate from high school, this opened the door to talk about how coming to class on time would help getting through Algebra I as a required class for graduation.

To me, this seems clear, but providing my students with the opportunities to make this connection themselves, set goals to come to class on time, create their own action plans, and take responsibility (e.g., set a phone alarm 3 minutes before class starts to make it on time to class) made all the difference! Learning my students' goals and reading their responses to the 12 SDLMI Student Questions also gave me more opportunities to create a more meaningful and engaging learning experience in my classroom. I have incorporated a variety of practices to enhance student learning (e.g., giving a 1-minute choice activity where students choose to do an extra problem, make a notecard of important steps, or update their calendar with plans to compete their assignment or study) to benefit and support all students in my class.

I see myself as a lifelong learner, and even with decades of experience, I am happy to model for my students that everyone should always be learning like I did by sharing my SDLMI goal each year (e.g., using a planner, eating more vegetables, exercising 5 days a week). It was fun to learn about my students and to have students ask about my progress and encourage me with my SDLMI goal.

-Annette F. McDonald, Lawrence Free State High School, Mathematics and SDLMI Teacher

FIGURE 7.1 My SDLMI Story: Self-Determination is the Missing Piece for ALL of MY Students. Copyright 2022 Kansas University Center on Developmental Disabilities

goals they, their families, and their communities value (Shogren et al., 2016).

In Chapter 5, we described a tiered supports framework for implementing the SDLMI that included three tiers of evidence-based, culturally sustainable, and universally designed instruction. Tiered supports provide increased intensities and individualization of support, including: (a) Tier 1 or universal instruction intended for *all* students, (b) Tier 2 or additional targeted instruction, and (c) Tier 3 or the most intensive support which can be individualized based on students' support needs

(Thurlow et al., 2020). An important common feature of tiered models is that the tiers are additive, meaning students with or without disabilities who are identified as needing additional instruction (e.g., Tier 2 or 3 supports) would receive this more targeted instruction in addition to receiving universal, Tier 1 instruction (Thurlow et al., 2020). Another important feature of tiered models of support is that support level does not equate to educational placement. In fact, as all students move through and receive more intensive instruction across tiers, all instruction can and should be embedded within inclusive, general education activities (Sailor, 2008).

In this chapter, we focus on how teachers and other professionals trained in the SDLMI can engage all students in inclusive contexts in the SDLMI as a Tier 1 or universal support. We share key Tier 1 implementation information as well as specific ways trained implementers can use the Teacher Objectives and Education Supports to engage students in answering the 12 Student Questions, utilizing natural supports in inclusive settings (e.g., peer supports). Finally, we share the voices of students and school leaders who have used the SDLMI to build self-determination and support students to achieve their learning goals in inclusive contexts.

Using the SDLMI in Inclusive Contexts: Key Implementation Information

When implemented as a universal or Tier 1 support in inclusive contexts, it is important to plan to make sure SDLMI implementation can be embedded in ongoing instruction (e.g., general education curriculum). While there are constant demands for more instructional time, using the SDLMI can provide students equitable opportunities to begin to engage and self-direct their learning. In the subsequent sections, we highlight key implementation information (e.g., SDLMI session frequency and length, focus of student goals) that SDLMI implementers consider when using the SDLMI inclusive contexts.

Whole-Class Implementation Schedule

Figure 7.2 shows a sample schedule for whole-class SDLMI instruction across one academic semester. SDLMI sessions are generally twice a week, for approximately 15 minutes, and target specific lesson objectives that are aligned with the 12 Student Questions and associated Teacher Objectives. As mentioned in Chapter 2, in school contexts, teachers engage students in the three phases of the SDLMI once per semester, meaning that students work through the entire SDLMI process in inclusive, general education classes twice during the school year, setting and working toward two goals. Two SDLMI cycles within a year supports repeated opportunities and experiences for students to practice setting goals, taking action to achieve those goals, and self-evaluating those goals or action plans. Each whole-class SDLMI lesson is approximately 15 minutes; however, teachers might decide to shorten or extend a particular lesson given students' support needs and other contextual factors (e.g., shortened school day schedule or low attendance or alternatively, high student engagement and more opportunities for student discussion). There also might be some adjustments to this schedule depending on school breaks, testing schedules, etc.; however, engaging students in lessons twice a week keeps goals and action plans at the forefront of their learning. Like other SDLMI implementation schedules described in Chapter 2, whole-class SDLMI instruction begins with the Self-Determination Inventory: Student Report (SDI:SR; Shogren & Wehmeyer, 2017) to support students in identifying their strengths and areas for growth across DECIDE, ACT, and BELIEVE. Then, students engage in a series of Preliminary Conversations to learn about and define self-determination for themselves. Teachers also introduce the SDLMI and key SDLMI-related terms (goal, action plan, self-evaluation). Students learn about the roles they take when using the SDLMI (self-advocate, self-directed learner, active learner) as well as the roles their teacher's take (instructor, facilitator, advocate).

As highlighted in Figure 7.2, whole-class instruction includes an opportunity for students to engage in the 12 Student

		Sample SDLMI Implementation Schedule – One Semester	
Week	Day	Mini-Lesson Topic	Mini-Lesson Notes
1	Wednesday, January 18th	WC #1 SDI:SR Pre-test	Take the SDI:SR online
	Friday, January 20th	WC #2 Introduction to Self-Determination	Introduction to Self-Determination
2	Wednesday, January 25th	WC #3 SDLMI	About the SDLMI
	Friday, January 27th	WC #4 Roles and SDLMI Key Terms	SDLMI Key Terms and Student/Teacher Roles
3	Wednesday, February 1st	WC #5 Student Questions 1-2	SQs 1 and 2 with a goal unrelated to core content
	Friday, February 3rd	WC #6 Student Questions 3-4	SQs 3 and 4 with a goal unrelated to core content
4	Wednesday, February 8th	WC #7 Student Questions 5-6	SQs 5 and 6 with a goal unrelated to core content
	Friday, February 10th	WC #8 Student Questions 7-8	SQs 7 and 8 with a goal unrelated to core content
5	Wednesday, February 15th	WC #9 Student Questions 9-10	SQs 9 and 10 with a goal unrelated to core content
	Monday, February 20th	WC #10 Student Questions 11-12	SQs 11 and 12 with a goal unrelated to core content
6	Wednesday, February 22nd	WC #11 Student Question 1	SQ 1: What do I want to learn? With core content goal
	Monday, February 26th	WC #12 Student Question 2	SQ 2: What do I know about it now? with core content goal
7	Wednesday, March 1st	WC #13 Student Question 3	SQ 3: What must change for me to learn what I don't know? with core content goal
	Friday, March 3rd	WC #14 Student Question 4	SQ 4: What can I do to make this happen? with core content goal
8	Wednesday, March 8th	WC #15 GAS Part 1	Write down goals individually using the GAS and then share, take GAS 1 online
	Friday, March 10th		No School- Professional Development Day
		Sample SDLMI Implementation Schedule (Continued)	
9	Wednesday, March 15th	WC #16 Student Question 5	SQ 5: What can I do to learn what I don't know? with core content goal
	Friday, March 17th	WC #17 Student Question 6	SQ 6" What could keep me from taking action? with core content goal
10	Wednesday, March 22nd		No School- Spring Break
	Friday, March 24th		No School- Spring Break
11	Wednesday, March 29th	WC #18 Progress Review	Review where you are in the planning process after a week off
	Friday, March 31st	WC #19 Student Question 7	SQ 7: What can I do to remove these barriers? with core content goal
12	Wednesday, April 5th	WC #20 Student Question 8	SQ 8: When will I take action? with core content goal
	Friday, April 7th		No School- Parent/Teacher Conferences
13	Wednesday, April 12th		No School- Parent/Teacher Conferences
	Friday, April 14th	WC #21 Student Question 9	SQ 9: What actions have I taken? with core content goal
14	Wednesday, April 19th	WC #22 Student Question 10	SQ 10: What barriers have been removed? with core content goal
	Friday, April 21st	WC #23 Student Question 11	SQ 11: What has changed about what I don't know? with core content goal
15	Wednesday, April 26th	WC #24 Student Question 12	SQ 12: Do I know what I want to know? with a core content goal
	Friday, April 28th	WC #25 SDI and GAS Part 2	Take the SDI:SR and GAS 2, reflection about the process, and planning next goal
16	Wednesday, May 3rd	WC #26 Celebration	Congratulations on working on your goal!

FIGURE 7.2 SDLMI Whole-Class Sample Implementation Schedule. Copyright 2022 Kansas University Center on Developmental Disabilities

Questions quickly (i.e., 2 Student Questions targeted per lesson) after Preliminary Conversations with a goal unrelated to content of the class and typically something fun and highly motivating (e.g., getting better at playing a specific video game, saving up for a car). This quick experience with the SDLMI has several benefits when supporting a whole class of students. First, going through the 12 Student Questions provides students with an opportunity to gain understanding of the three-phase process of the SDLMI in a "practice trial" with a self-selected goal that is not specifically related to a core content area and is instead associated with individual areas of interest. Second, students are more likely to engage in conversations around topics that are more interesting to them individually instead of a content area as they first use the SDLMI, supporting the development of a trusting relationship with their teacher. Third, this strategy allows the teacher to explain the SDLMI learning process with a low-stakes goal before starting a content-specific goal. Teachers should also encourage students to discuss their goal area interests unrelated to core content with their family to promote partnerships and communication between students, families, and teachers. After progressing through the three phases of the SDLMI with a practice goal in an area of interest unrelated to the content area, students are ready to begin the SDLMI with a core content goal. Following the quick SDLMI "practice trial" with a goal unrelated to core content, students are ready to be presented with "goal buckets" (described in Chapter 2) as they begin Phase 1: Set a Goal.

Whole-Class SDLMI Goal Buckets

When implementing the SDLMI class-wide, teachers can select broad goal areas that they would target through their instruction (e.g., preparedness, note-taking, specific content strategies related to the subject area–math, science, English Language Arts), and support students to select one goal area and develop an individualized learning goal within that goal area. For example, if a student selects the goal bucket of preparedness, then their specific goal might be "I will make sure to bring the book we are reading in English Language Arts class every day and put it in my backpack every night after I read so I don't forget." In this context, the overall goals for instruction are still being targeted (e.g., reading a book and identifying key themes), but students take more responsibility and ownership over the steps they need to take to achieve that curricular goal by setting a personal and specific learning goal. Students are given the opportunity to reflect on their current status related to the goal areas. SDLMI implementers support them to think about and identify a specific goal that they would like to target as they progress through the three phases of the SDLMI. Students can then, after they achieve their goal, select another goal related to this broad area or a different area to continue their learning. This way, the teacher enables students to individualize their goal given self-identified strengths and areas of need and also narrows the wide range of goal areas making goal setting and evaluation manageable across all the students in the class. If none of the goal areas apply to a given student, the teacher can discuss options for further individualization of the goal area and subsequent specific learning goal with the student.

Whole-Class SDLMI Engagement Strategies

Using the SDLMI with a whole-class offers opportunities to leverage natural supports and engage students in supporting each other's goal setting and attainment processes. For example, teachers can prompt students to get into small groups based on their goal bucket selection (e.g., note-taking) and discuss what barriers or supports they have identified as they engage in Phase 2: Take Action so they can learn from each other. Also, students can serve as helpful accountability checkers for each other (e.g., one student reminding a peer "Don't forget to review the flashcards we made today because we have a quiz tomorrow"). Teachers should continually check with students to ensure peer supports are mutually beneficial. The ultimate goal of whole-class SDLMI instruction is to have a community of goal setters in a classroom working toward their goals with everyone benefiting from support from each other. For example, Figure 7.3 highlights

SDLMI Goal K-W-L Resource

Directions:

1. Complete the **Initial Thoughts** sections below and reflect on what you (1) know about your goal now, (2) still want to know about your goal, and (3) have learned while working to achieve your goal.
2. **Discuss your Initial thoughts** in small groups and write down in the sections below as you share.
3. Complete the **Final Thoughts** sections below and consider what you are thinking about for the next time you work through the SDLMI.

	What do I **know** about my goal now?	What do I **want to know** about my goal?	What have I **learned** about my process to achieve my goal?
Initial thoughts			
Discuss thoughts			
Final thoughts			

FIGURE 7.3 SDLMI Whole-Class Student Question 9 Resource Example. Copyright 2022 Kansas University Center on Developmental Disabilities

a SDLMI resource teachers use when supporting students to answer Student Question 9: What actions have I taken? This resource prompts students to self-evaluate their progress toward goal achievement (Teacher Objective 9a) by asking them to record their initial thoughts about what they know about their goal after working on it, what they want to know about their goal still, and what they have learned about their process to achieve their goal. After documenting their initial thoughts, students are then prompted to discuss their reflections in small groups and record notes as they discuss with peers. Finally, the resource prompts students to record any additional reflections they have after discussing with their peers.

Using the SDLMI in inclusive contexts has the power to create an environment for all students, including students with and without disabilities, to set and work toward goals they, their families, and their communities value. In Chapter 9, we describe specific supports to engage students with complex communication needs in the SDLMI, but it is important to note that all strategies highlighted can and should be used in inclusive contexts providing equitable opportunities for all students to become self-determined.

References

Lombardi, A., Freeman, J., & Rifenbark, G. (2018). Modeling college and career readiness for adolescents with and without disabilities: A bifactor approach. *Exceptional Children, 84*(2), 159–176. https://doi.org/10.1177/0014402917731557

Raley, S. K., Shogren, K. A., Rifenbark, G. G., Lane, K. L., & Pace, J. R. (2021). The impact of the Self-Determined Learning Model of Instruction on student self-determination in inclusive, secondary classrooms. *Remedial and Special Education, 42*(6), 363–373. https://doi.org/10.1177/0741932520984842

Rowe, D. A., Mazzotti, V. L., Fowler, C. H., Test, D. W., Mitchell, V. J., Clark, K. A., Holzberg, D., Owens, T. L., Rusher, D., Seaman-Tullis, R. L., Gushanas, C. M., Castle, H., Chang, W.-H., Voggt, A., Kwiatek, S., & Dean, C. (2021). Updating the secondary transition research base:

Evidence- and research-based practices in functional skills. *Career Development and Transition for Exceptional Individuals, 44*(1), 28–46. https://doi.org/10.1177/2165143420958674

Sailor, W. (2008). Access to the general curriculum: Systems change or tinker some more? *Research and Practice for Persons with Severe Disabilities, 34*(1), 249–257. https://doi.org/10.2511/rpsd.33.4.249

Shogren, K. A., Hicks, T. A., Raley, S. K., Pace, J. R., Rifenbark, G. G., & Lane, K. L. (2021). Student and teacher perceptions of goal attainment during intervention with the Self-Determined Learning Model of Instruction. *The Journal of Special Education, 55*(2), 101–112. https://doi.org/10.1177/0022466920950264

Shogren, K. A., & Wehmeyer, M. L. (2017). *Self-Determination Inventory: Student-Report.* Kansas University Center on Developmental Disabilities.

Shogren, K. A., Wehmeyer, M. L., & Lane, K. L. (2016). Embedding interventions to promote self-determination within multi-tiered systems of supports. *Exceptionality, 24*(4), 213–224. https://doi.org/10.1080/09362835.2015.1064421

Thurlow, M. L., Ghere, G., Lazarus, S. S., & Liu, K. K. (2020). *MTSS for all: Including students with the most significant cognitive disabilities.* National Center on Educational Outcomes; TIES Center. https://nceo.umn.edu/docs/OnlinePubs/NCEOBriefMTSS.pdf

Ward, M. J. (2005). An historical perspective of self-determination in special education: Accomplishments and challenges. *Research and Practice for Persons with Severe Disabilities, 30*(3), 108–112. https://doi.org/10.2511/rpsd.30.3.108

8

Transition Planning and the SDLMI

We're not here to crush students' dreams as they prepare for the transition to adulthood – instead, we want to empower them to be self-determined as they set and work towards goals they identify as important in their lives with our support along the way!

(Kristin Luetschwager and MiQuela Brown, junior high school special education and SDLMI teachers)

You've learned about the Self-Determined Learning Model of Instruction (SDLMI) and its core components (Chapter 2), its research base (Chapter 3), and ways it can be implemented using a tiered support framework (Chapter 5), ensuring all students get the supports they need to learn and use self-determination abilities, skills, and attitudes. In Chapter 6, you learned about infusing culturally responsive teaching practices into the SDLMI to ensure that all students' cultural identities and funds of knowledge are valued, celebrated, and integrated into setting goals (Phase 1), creating action plans to achieve those goals (Phase 2), and evaluating progress (Phase 3). In Chapter 7, you learned about ways that the SDLMI can be used in inclusive contexts to support *all* students to build self-determination. Now, it is time learn about ways the SDLMI can be used to support planning for the transition from school to adult life, building on and enhancing opportunities for self-determination

DOI: 10.4324/9781003214373-8

instruction provided in inclusive, core content classrooms. Transition planning is essential for all students and is increasingly being targeted in secondary general education curricula for all students and the materials and strategies described in this chapter can be used for all students. However, for young people with disabilities approaching adulthood, the importance of transition planning has long been recognized as essential to changing persistent disparities in postschool outcomes (Shogren & Wehmeyer, 2020). Supports for transition planning are a key part of effective secondary special education services and supports, and self-determination should be a key focus in these efforts. After all, it's the student's future!

The Individuals with Disabilities Education Improvement Act (IDEIA) of 2004 requires all students with disabilities who have an Individualized Education Program (IEP) at age 16 have access to transition planning, which is defined as a:

> coordinated set of activities for a child with a disability that (a) is designed to be within a results-oriented process focused on improving the academic and functional achievement of the child with a disability to facilitate the child's movement from school to post school activities, including post-secondary education, vocational education, integrated and supported employment, continuing and adult education, adult services, independent living or community participation and (b) is based on the individual child's unique needs, taking into account the child's strengths, preferences, and interests …

Goals for postsecondary education, employment, and community living and participation are essential to effective transition planning, and this is where the SDLMI can be used to support students to set goals that drive transition planning. This creates more opportunities for young people to practice and refine their self-determination abilities and skills, particularly when they are also learning about them as part of the general education curriculum and universal, Tier 1 self-determination supports.

Using the SDLMI in Transition Planning: Key Implementation Information

To support teachers to use the SDLMI to support transition planning, specific materials and resources have been developed guiding how the core SDLMI components (Student Questions, Teacher Objectives, and Educational Supports) can be used to enable young people to set and go after transition goals, in collaboration with their families, friends, and community networks (Shogren et al., 2019). These materials include 22 lessons organized around the three SDLMI phases (Phase 1: Set a Goal; Phase 2: Take Action; Phase 3: Adjust Goal or Plan) with a focus on integrating the SDLMI into transition planning activities and supporting students to self-direct the process of setting goals related to moving from school to adult roles and responsibilities. The SDLMI Transition Planning can be implemented with small groups or during 1-1 instruction focused on transition as a Tier 2 support. How the SDLMI Transition Planning is used should be based on student needs and available instruction time. SDLMI Transition Planning can also be combined with other curricula that provide more targeted and intensive transition planning instruction as a Tier 3 support (e.g., Whose Future Is It or the Self-Directed IEP; Burke et al., 2019; Raley et al., in press).

Transition Planning Implementation Schedule

The 22 lessons for SDLMI Transition Planning allow for more in-depth and targeted instruction compared to the lessons developed to support SDLMI implementation in inclusive general education classrooms you read about in Chapter 7. Each SDLMI Transition Planning lesson takes approximately 30-45 minutes to implement and targets key objectives relevant to building self-determination skills and abilities to support transition-related goal setting and attainment. Students work through one cycle of the SDLMI in approximately 16-weeks or one academic semester, with sessions twice a week. A sample SDLMI Transition Planning implementation schedule is provided in Figure 8.1. This enables the SDLMI to be an iterative process, repeated semester after

		Sample SDLMI Transition Planning Implementation Schedule – One Semester	
Week	Day	Mini-Lesson Topic	Mini-Lesson Notes
1	Wednesday, September 16	#1 SDI:SR Pre-test	TP1 Self-Determination Inventory: Student Report (SDI:SR) Pre-test
	Friday, September 18	#2 Preliminary Conversation	TP2 Introduction to Self-Determination
2	Wednesday, September 23	#3 Preliminary Conversation	TP3 Goals
	Friday, September 25	#4 Preliminary Conversation	TP4 SDLMI, Roles, and Key Terms
3	Wednesday, September 30	#5 Phase 1: Set a Goal	TP5 Student Question 1: *What do I want to learn?*
	Friday, October 2	#6 Phase 1: Set a Goal	TP6 Student Question 2: *What do I know about it now?*
	Wednesday, October 7	#7 Phase 1: Set a Goal	TP7 Student Question 3: *What must change for me to learn what I don't know?*
4	Friday, October 9	#8 Phase 1: Set a Goal	TP8 Student Question 4: What can I do to make this happen?
	Wednesday, October 14	#9 GAS Part 1	TP9 Goal Attainment Scaling (GAS) Part 1: Set Your Goal
5	Friday, October 16	#10 Phase 2: Take Action	TP10 Student Question 5: *What can I do to learn what I don't know?*
	Wednesday, October 21	#11 Phase 2: Take Action	TP11 Student Question 6: *What could keep me from taking action?*
6	Friday, October 23		No School- Professional Development Day
	Wednesday, October 28	#12 Mid-Phase 2 Check-in	TP12 Mid-Phase 2 Check-in
7	Friday, October 30	#13 Phase 2: Take Action	TP13 Student Question 7: *What can I do to remove these barriers?*
	Wednesday, November 4	#14 Phase 2: Take Action	TP14 Student Question 8: *When will I take action?*
8	Friday, November 6	#15 End of Phase 2 Check-In	TP15 End of Phase 2 Check-in
	Wednesday, November 11		No School- Professional Development Day
9	Friday, November 13	#16 Phase 3: Adjust Goal or Plan	TP16 Student Question 9: *What actions have I taken?*
	Wednesday, November 18	#17 Phase 3: Adjust Goal or Plan	TP17 Student Question 10: *What barriers have been removed?*
10	Friday, November 20	#18 Phase 3: Adjust Goal or Plan	TP18 Student Question 11: *What has changed about what I don't know?*
	Wednesday, November 25		No School- Fall Break
11	Friday, November 27		No School- Fall Break
	Wednesday, December 2	#19 Phase 3: Adjust Goal or Plan	TP19 Student Question 12: *Do I know what I want to know?*
12	Friday, December 4	#20 GAS Part 2	TP20 Goal Attainment Scaling (GAS) Part 2: Indicate Goal Attainment
	Wednesday, December 9	#21 SDI:SR Post-test	TP21 Self-Determination Inventory: Student Report (SDI:SR) Post-test
13	Friday, December 11	#22 Celebration!	TP22 Congratulations on working on your goal!

FIGURE 8.1 SDLMI Transition Planning Sample Implementation Schedule. Copyright 2022 Kansas University Center on Developmental Disabilities

semester, creating opportunities for young people to continue to refine and advance their goals for after high school across multiple domains, including postsecondary education, employment, and community living and participation.

Each SDLMI Transition Planning lesson has accompanying materials, such as a lesson plan, PowerPoint, and when appropriate a resource that educators can use with students to support them in answering the Student Question and documenting their progress. Figure 8.2 highlights a sample resource educators and students use during the SDLMI Transition Planning lesson focused on Student Question 4: What can I do to make this happen? This resource supports transition-age students in setting a measurable, observable, and specific goal related to transition planning. These materials can and should be adapted to each teacher's style of teaching and student support needs (Burke et al., 2019). Chapter 9, for example, will highlight ways that SDLMI materials can be individualized for students with complex communication needs.

Transition Planning Goal Buckets

One major focus of the SDLMI Transition Planning is to establish a clear emphasis on goals that advance students' movement toward the roles and responsibilities they want to take on after high school. For this reason, the goal buckets for SDLMI Transition Planning focus around key transition domains: postsecondary education, employment, and community participation. These goal buckets enable teachers to guide students in self-directing the process of setting goals while still ensuring the goals relate to transition planning. For example, students who select the goal bucket of employment could focus on, depending on where they are in their process of identifying their plans for postschool employment, exploring career interests, identifying skills or training needed for a given job, shadowing someone who has a job they are interested in, or seeking internship or work experiences. Similarly, for students who select the postsecondary education goal bucket, goals could focus on exploring college options and resources, including different types of colleges and training programs, disability supports at colleges and

SDLMI
Self-Determined Learning
Model of Instruction

Practicing with Goals

Directions:

1. Review the definitions of measurable, observable, and specific in the blue boxes below.
2. Take a look at the non-examples for each and then write or type in an example of a goal that is measurable, observable, or specific.
3. Based on your goal, write a goal that is measurable, observable, and specific.

Every goal should be...

Measurable

Something you can count or quantify

Non-example: "Do research on careers I might want." How can you measure that?

Example: _____

Observable

Something you can see/hear and say whether or not it happened

Non-example: "Learn about careers." How can you observe that?

Example: _____

Specific

Something clearly identified and defined

Non-example: "Go to a career fair." Is this clearly defined?
Example: _____

Now take your goal and try to make it measurable, observable, and specific!

_____

FIGURE 8.2 SDLMI Transition Planning Student Question 4 Resource Example. Copyright 2022 Kansas University Center on Developmental Disabilities

universities, application requirements, and what a typical day looks like for a college student.

Students may work within the same goal bucket as they use the SDLMI across semesters, developing more targeted and specific SDLMI goals or they may work across goal buckets, exploring employment options one semester and exploring options for where to live in the community another semester. The process of selecting goal buckets can and should be individualized to students' interests, support needs, and transition planning priorities. It is also important to recognize that part of the SDLMI process is supporting exploration of these areas. Changes in goals and priorities happen with iterations of the SDLMI – remember that the focus should be on enabling exploration and using this to drive learning, not ruling out any initial goals as unattainable or unrealistic. For example, the SDLMI provides a process to enable students to explore careers that might have a low probability (e.g., professional football player or actor) but are still worthy of learning about, particularly to guide ongoing refinement of interests and alignment of strengths with career options. Figure 8.3, *My SDLMI Story,* highlights how Kristin Luetschwager and MiQuela Brown, junior high school special education and SDLMI teachers, saw the SDLMI shift their approach to enabling students to self-direct their goal-setting process.

Transition Planning SDLMI Engagement Strategies

As mentioned, the SDLMI Transition Planning materials follow the same general schedule and integrate the same SDLMI core components you learned about in Chapter 7. However, SDLMI Transition Planning has more intensive supports and resources targeting key transition domains and planning activities. For example, during Phase 1: Set a Goal, to support students in answering Student Question 1: What do I want to learn?, a teacher may engage students in a variety of transition-related assessments, such as career interest inventories or transition planning inventories (Patton & Tran, 2020). This can serve multiple purposes, including supporting students in identifying their interests, as well as providing information for students with disabilities to bring into their IEP and transition planning meetings, informing the development of transition supports and services aligned with students' SDLMI goals.

For example, to support students to identify their goal at the end of Phase 1, teachers can support students to narrow their various areas of interest within their goal bucket and identify things they would like to explore in greater depth through the SDLMI. In the early stages of transition planning, for example, students might focus on surveying resources available in their

MiQuela and Kristin first learned about the SDLMI through a pilot program the Arkansas Department of Education started during the 2021–2022 school year focused on scaling-up use of the SDLMI across the state. As they described, "what drew us to the SDLMI was how it could support the 8th graders we work with to be successful in transition planning as a part of their IEPs." From their perspective, transitions happen across the life course (elementary to junior high, high school to adulthood, etc.) so using the SDLMI made sense for their students aged 15 going on 16. MiQuela and Kristin saw that using the SDLMI would give them a chance to support students in starting to think about their future and planning their pathway to graduation and their high school schedules. Below are their SDLMI stories!

MiQuela engaged eight 8th grade students in the SDLMI and they were *all* interested in athletic-related goals. They all had dreams of playing professional football or basketball. She didn't want to crush their dreams of playing in the NFL or NBA; instead, she suggested they also talk about what their back-up plan was. They talked about how at times, players end up hurt and can no longer play sports, so what would they want to do then? They also talked about how in order to play in professional college sports, students would have to go to college. In college, athletes have a major of study and attend classes, not just play their sport of choice. During a SDLMI Phase 1 lesson focused on students setting a goal, MiQuela pulled up the Arkansas Razorback football team roster online to look at what some athletes had chosen as their major to give the students an idea of what majors different players had chosen. These conversations supported the students to think about more of their interests beyond athletics, opening up opportunities for them to get excited about transition goals related to researching college majors. Some students even started looking at technical jobs instead of careers in professional sports, just in case they were injured. So, goals related to being an NFL or NBA player weren't labeled as unrealistic (Who can decide that?), but MiQuela focused on how she could embrace students' goals and support and learn from them as they worked through SDLMI phases.

Kristin engaged 8th grade students with a range of support needs (intellectual disability, learning disabilities, etc.) in the SDLMI. She found the SDLMI opened up a pathway for conversations on what students were interested in and then a process for students to set a goal, create an action plan to achieve that goal, and evaluate their progress to inform their next transition goal. Two students started with career goals in mind already: one to be an architect and the other a commercial truck driver. Other students were not as sure about their futures and that was okay too. Using their SDI Reports, Kristin and her SDLMI students collaboratively identified their self-determination strengths and areas for growth across DECIDE, ACT, and BELIEVE. From there, students were able to not only have conversations with Kristin, but with one another about their self-determination strengths and next steps. Kristin found that using the SDLMI enabled students to walk away with a better understanding of who they are, their self-determination, and what steps they could take to work toward transition goals. In MiQuela's and Kristin's words, "We can't wait to see these students continue to use the SDLMI as transition to high school and beyond!"

—MiQuela Brown and Kristin Luetschwager, Batesville Junior High School, Special Education and SDLMI Teachers

FIGURE 8.3 Our SDLMI Story: Who Decides What is an Unrealistic Goal? Copyright 2022 Kansas University Center on Developmental Disabilities

communities to support learning about careers in a specific area, like sports management or in the restaurant industry. This provides a natural time for students to be supported to communicate with their family and share what they are learning, as well as get input on what their family thinks about their goals and support needs. Teachers can use SDLMI Transition Planning resources focused on enhancing student-family-school communication around SDLMI goals and transition planning.

During SDLMI Transition Planning instruction, students use the Self-Determination Inventory described in Chapter 4 and Goal Attainment Scaling (GAS) to reflect on their self-determination and their expectations for attaining their goals. This can guide students as they create action plans in Phase 2 to make progress toward their goals. This creates natural opportunities for celebration of steps that students take toward transition goals, and ongoing reflection by the student in what else they need to learn as they prepare to move from school to adult roles and responsibilities (Phase 3). This reflection may also create opportunities for discussing barriers to meaningful adult outcomes that are experienced by people with disabilities, and discussions about systemic issues that need to be changed to create equitable opportunities for all people to thrive in adulthood. Talking about systemic issues and incorporating learning about racial and disability justice can be a highly impactful way to advance culturally responsive teaching practices (Chapter 6). For example, disabled leaders from the local community can serve as mentors leveraging funds of knowledge held in the disability community, partnering with students as they continue to refine their goals, preparing for the next iteration of the SDLMI. At any phase in SDLMI instruction, disabled leaders can share real-life examples of advocacy in the community. Students can share their learning with others, including their families, teachers, IEP team members, and peers and mentors. Building mentorship and access to the disability and cultural justice community can be an essential way to enable students to build community networks that will support them in enacting what they learn through the SDLMI in school and beyond.

References

Burke, K. M., Shogren, K. A., Antosh, A. A., LaPlante, T., & Masterson, L. H. (2019). Implementing the SDLMI with students with significant support needs during transition planning. *Career Development and Transition for Exceptional Individuals*, *43*(2), 115–121. https://doi.org/10.1177/2165143419887858

Individuals With Disabilities Education Improvement Act, H. R. 1350, 108th Congress. 2004.

Patton, J. R., & Tran, L. M. (2020). Transition assessment. In K. A. Shogren & M. L. Wehmeyer (Eds.), *Handbook of adolescent transition education for youth with disabilities* (2nd ed.). Routledge.

Raley, S. K., Hagiwara, M., Burke, K. M., Kiblen, J. C., & Shogren, K. A. (in press). Supporting all students to be self-determined: Using the Self-Determined Learning Model of Instruction within multi-tiered systems of supports. *Inclusive Practices*.

Shogren, K. A., Burke, K. M., & Raley, S. K. (2019). *SDLMI teacher's guide supplement: Implementing the SDLMI to enhance transition planning*. Kansas University Center on Developmental Disabilities.

Shogren, K. A., & Wehmeyer, M. L. (Eds.). (2020). *Handbook of adolescent transition education for youth with disabilities* (2nd ed.). Routledge.

9

SDLMI and People with Complex Communication Needs

People with complex communication needs have the right to live self-determined lives. They don't need to "earn" opportunities to build self-determination—it should be a given.

(Sarah Brady, Special Education and SDLMI Teacher,
WISH Community and Academy Schools)

As you have learned, the Self-Determined Learning Model of Instruction (SDLMI) can be used in diverse contexts to support *all* youth and young adults with and without disabilities to work toward goals they identify as meaningful in their lives. Chapter 5 described how the SDLMI can be used within a multi-tiered systems of supports (MTSS) framework to create inclusive environments that enable all students to build self-determination abilities, skills, and attitudes (e.g., decision making, goal setting, problem solving, self-awareness). Students with complex communication needs should always be included in Tier 1 instruction and might need specific Tier 2 and 3 supports to enhance their self-determined learning and engage at Tier 1 (Shogren et al., 2016; Thurlow et al., 2020). With knowledge of how the SDLMI can be used in inclusive contexts as a Tier 1 or universal support (Chapter 7) and in specific contexts like transition planning for more intensive or Tier 2 instruction (Chapter 8), this chapter focuses on how to use the SDLMI across tiers to support students

DOI: 10.4324/9781003214373-9

with complex communication needs to set and work toward goals. These strategies will also benefit other students with extensive supports needs and who need individualized supports to engage in SDLMI instruction.

Students who use or would benefit from access to augmentative and alternative communication (AAC) supports are often referred to as having complex communication needs (Beukelman & Mirenda, 2013). A student might use a combination of unaided forms of AAC (e.g., sign language), low-tech aided AAC (e.g., picture-based communication systems), and/or high-tech aided AAC systems such as speech-generating devices (Beukelman & Mirenda, 2013). Students with complex communication needs are often marginalized in school contexts and provided limited access to self-determination instruction, opportunities, and supports, particularly when they do not have access to needed communication supports. Because supports for communication are a consideration for many teachers of students with extensive support needs, strategies to integrate unaided, low-tech, and high-tech AAC into SDLMI instruction can be essential to provide equitable access and opportunities to build self-determination. For example, special education teachers of students with intellectual disability engaged in state-wide implementation of the SDLMI (e.g., Shogren, Burke, et al., 2018; Shogren et al., 2019), described the two primary barriers they encountered in implementing self-determination. These barriers were instructional time ($n = 9$) and needing additional support with aligning instruction with student's support needs ($n = 4$; Raley et al., 2020). As one teacher described related to aligning instruction with students' support needs, "It's very difficult for those that have more [extensive support needs]. However, for one of my students I am focusing on one thing for a long period of time so it is doable!" This highlights how extended time to review content and integrate communication supports can enhance SDLMI instruction, but also necessitates individualized scheduling and planning for more intensive supports. With these supports, in this state-wide SDLMI implementation, educators consistently identified the SDLMI as supporting student outcomes. One teacher said, "I am beginning to see changes in our students as they learn more about themselves, their needs, and ability to be self-determined." Reflections from teachers using the SDLMI with students with complex communication needs highlight that there are barriers to address, but there are also solutions that can enable students with complex communication needs to receive equitable opportunities to build self-determination.

Using the SDLMI with Students with Complex Communication Needs: Key Implementation Information

To support educators in using the SDLMI with students with complex communication needs, specific materials and resources have been developed guiding how the core SDLMI components (Student Questions, Teacher Objectives, and Educational Supports) can be used to enable young people with complex communication needs to set and go after goals. In particular, developers of the SDLMI created a supplement to the SDLMI Teacher's Guide (Shogren, Raley, et al., 2018) with specific strategies and examples for using the SDLMI with students with complex communication needs, the *Teacher's Guide Supplement: Supporting Students with Complex Communication Needs to Engage with the SDLMI* (Shogren & Burke, 2019). This supplement includes instructional supports and examples that show how the Student Questions can be made accessible and meaningful for students with complex communication needs, with reminders to teachers that they will likely need to modify activities and materials based on their student's unique strengths, beliefs, values, and instructional needs and the specific forms of AAC that they need and benefit from. For example, the Teacher Objectives associated with Student Question 1 (What do I want to learn?) focus on enabling the student to initiate identifying what they want to learn or improve on. To do this, teachers of students with complex communication needs can support the student to identify their specific strengths and instructional needs and then communicate and prioritize those needs. For students with complex communication needs, teachers might find that using visual supports to see what students identify as areas of interest (e.g., images of possible goal buckets) might be helpful. These images support teachers in making the concept of goal bucket selection more concrete. Images can be created by taking pictures of the student during various class activities (e.g., participating in a group project, completing class-work) or while sampling employment or recreation areas (e.g., visiting a job site to identify job expectations, finding an after-school activity to participate in) and using these images for the students to choose from.

For some students with complex communication needs, AAC may be an essential part of identifying what they want to learn or improve on. For students with complex communication needs who use AAC, teachers might plan ahead and load images into a student's AAC device reflecting SDLMI lesson content and ensure students have access to their AAC device throughout the school day so they can communicate about their goal (e.g., "Going to woodworking class is my SDLMI goal"). Figure 9.1 highlights several examples of ways teachers can use pictures to support students to answer SDLMI Student Question 1. Each of the images reflects different ways to pose Student Question 1, based on a student's preferred vocabulary that still reflects the intent of the question ("What do I want to learn?"). We also introduced alternate phrasing in Chapter 3, Figure 2.3. The four images highlight ways that pictures, words, and images can be used to allow students to express their interests and what they want to learn about as they seek to identify their SDLMI goal. These pictures can be oriented around academic domains as you learned about in Chapter 7 or transition outcomes (e.g., employ-ment, postsecondary education, community participation) as you learned about in Chapter 8. This can enable students with com-plex communication needs to participate and access content with their peers with and without disabilities across content areas.

Teachers might also use graphic organizers as visual sup-ports in combination with images or pictures to enable students with complex communication needs to communicate their back-ground knowledge about their selected SDLMI goal bucket or goal. For example, to support students in answering Student Question 2 (What do I know about it now?) and to meet the asso-ciated Teacher Objectives, educators can enable students with complex communication needs to write, draw, or select images to

FIGURE 9.1 Example of Visual Supports for Student Question 1: What Do I Want to Learn? Copyright 2022 Kansas University Center on Developmental Disabilities

represent what they know about their goal now. Figure 9.2 shows a teacher-created "T"-chart that has the SDLMI goal bucket at the top, and the following questions on the left side: "What am I currently doing?"; "What are things that support me to do this now?"; and "What are the barriers I face now?" These prompts

Goal Area: Learning about careers working with animals

Question	Answer
What am I currently doing?	*I take care of my pets.*
What are things that support me to do this now?	*I volunteer at the humane society.*
What are the barriers I face now?	*I need to learn about careers with animals.*

FIGURE 9.2 Example Graphic Organizer with Visual Supports for Student Question 2: What Do I Know about it Now? Copyright 2022 Kansas University Center on Developmental Disabilities

are the same questions from the Student Question 2 SDLMI Transition Planning materials and the T-chart supports instruction by separating information into columns. In this example, the student's response to Student Question 1 was that they wanted to learn about careers working with animals. And, the images that were selected by teachers reflect images that support the student in continuing to reflect on what they know now. Students can use eye gaze, circle desired options, or write/draw/copy the image on the right side of the T-chart to meaningfully respond to Student Question 2. You might have noted that these examples, and those highlighted in the SDLMI Teacher's Guide CCN supplement, are intensified Educational Supports. This reflects how Educational Supports are meant to be used to enable all students, including those with complex communication needs, to engage with the SDLMI Teacher Objectives and Student Questions.

Intensifying SDLMI Educational Supports for Students with CCN

In Chapter 2, you learned that SDLMI implementers utilize Educational Supports (e.g., goal-setting instruction, self-management instruction) to meet Teacher Objectives and enable students to learn the skills needed to answer the Student Questions and self-direct learning as they work toward goals. For some students with complex communication needs, intensifying Educational Supports is needed so educators can meet the Teacher Objectives and enable the student with complex communication needs to answer the targeted Student Question. For example, in Figure 9.1, the teacher intensified the Educational Supports of communication and decision-making instruction by including pictures and phrases in the student's AAC system to enable the student to communicate their preferences, interests, beliefs, and values and prioritize needs, meeting the Teacher Objectives for Student Question 1. This could occur in inclusive general education classrooms as part of Tier 1 supports or could also be provided during Tier 2 or 3 instruction, when students need more time to learn, practice, and reflect on their goals and interests. Similarly, in Figure 9.2, the teacher decided to intensify the use of awareness and self-advocacy instruction through the SDLMI Educational Supports to enable the student to gather information about opportunities, barriers, and supports in their identified goal bucket. It is important to note that it may take some time to implement intensified Educational Supports like the T-chart highlighted in Figure 9.2 and empower students to answer Student Questions. This is where Tier 2 and 3 supports can come into play, and teachers can adjust their SDLMI implementation schedule to schedule activities over several instructional sessions. See Figure 9.3 to learn more about Sarah Brady's *SDLMI*

I first heard about the SDLMI as a part of a pilot project the middle school I teach at engaged in to support *all* students, including students with CCN, to build self-determination. When I first heard about the SDLMI from school leaders, I really saw how it aligns with my teaching because often times students with CCN are seen as having to "earn their right" to learn in inclusive settings instead of us changing the environment to meet their support needs. At our school, we are committed to all students learning in fully inclusive settings with special education supports and services delivered using a push-in model. The SDLMI seemed like another way to support students with CCN in being successful in our inclusive classrooms by empowering them to set and work toward goals they identify as meaningful so we can structure classrooms that support their autonomy and self-determination.

I used the SDLMI in an advisory class, like homeroom, for middle school students. Advisory class took place during the first 30 minutes of the school day, which provided a more flexible time when we could use SDLMI and included all students together. In this advisory class, I co-implemented the SDLMI with a general education teacher and engaged two students with CCN, a couple other students with Individualized Education Programs (IEPs) but not CCN, and many students without disabilities. During the SDLMI lessons in advisory class, my general education co-teacher and I really focused on giving real examples of goals we set and work towards to engage students in whole-group activities. Outside of advisory class, I also supported one of the students with CCN individually in a class designed to provide more intensive support. During this class, I was able to provide additional SDLMI Educational Supports and individualized instruction that was a deeper extension of activity we engaged in during advisory class. For example, to support this student's understanding of SDLMI key terms (e.g., goal, barrier, plan) during a Preliminary Conversations lesson, I modified a resource we used in class by adding pictures for each key term and examples to talk through together. I really wanted this to be engaging for the student so I used examples he would be excited about like my example of having a *plan* to take my dog, Violet, to the park every day after school. He got to know my dog over a year of distance learning and seeing her in my video background often so I knew that was a way to connect and support him learning SDLMI key terms in addition to what he was learning in advisory class.

I can't emphasize the importance of using the SDLMI over and over again to support all students, including students with CCN, to build self-determination. Because I used the SDLMI for just one semester with that advisory class, some students needed more time to build their application of the concept of setting goals and what it looks like to follow through on those goals. So, many sure this happens repeatedly and is weaved in throughout the life course is critical, especially for students with CCN.

—Sarah Brady, Special Education and SDLMI Teacher,
WISH Community and Academy Schools

FIGURE 9.3 My SDLMI Story: Empowering Students with CCN to Self-Direct the SDLMI. Copyright 2022 Kansas University Center on Developmental Disabilities

Story and how she used the SDLMI in inclusive settings to support all students, including students with complex communication needs, to set and work towards goals. She describes how she intensified Educational Supports with real-world and engaging examples to connect with her students. These examples highlight how teachers using the SDLMI with students with complex communication needs are using the same SDLMI core components (Student Questions, Teacher Objectives, Educational Supports), but how individualized decision making is needed to intensity supports and instruction based on students' support needs and their goals for the future. Remember too, that students can and should be involved in selecting the communication supports and the images used—students are the experts in their learning and supports!

References

Beukelman, D., & Mirenda, P. (2013). *Augmentative and alternative communication: Supporting children and adults with complex communication needs* (4th ed.). Paul H. Brookes Publishing Co.

Raley, S. K., Burke, K. M., Hagiwara, M., Shogren, K. A., Wehmeyer, M. L., & Kurth, J. A. (2020). The Self-Determined Learning Model of Instruction and students with extensive support needs in inclusive settings. *Intellectual and Developmental Disabilities*, *58*(1), 82–90. https://doi.org/10.1352/1934-9556-58.1.82

Shogren, K. A., & Burke, K. M. (2019). *Teacher's guide supplement: Supporting students with complex communication needs to engage with the SDLMI.* Kansas University Center on Developmental Disabilities.

Shogren, K. A., Burke, K. M., Anderson, M. A., Antosh, A. A., Wehmeyer, M. L., LaPlante, T., & Shaw, L. A. (2018). Evaluating the differential impact of interventions to promote self-determination and goal attainment for transition-age youth with intellectual disability. *Research and Practice for Persons with Severe Disabilities*, *43*(3), 165–180. https://doi.org/10.1177/1540796918779775

Shogren, K. A., Burke, K. M., Antosh, A. A., Wehmeyer, M. L., LaPlante, T., Shaw, L. A., & Raley, S. K. (2019). Impact of the Self-Determined Learning Model of Instruction on self-determination and goal attainment in adolescents with intellectual disability. *Journal of Disability Policy Studies*, *30*(1), 22–34. https://doi.org/10.1177/1044207318792178

Shogren, K. A., Raley, S. K., Burke, K. M., & Wehmeyer, M. L. (2018). *The Self-Determined Learning Model of Instruction: Teacher's guide*. Kansas University Center on Developmental Disabilities.

Shogren, K. A., Wehmeyer, M. L., & Lane, K. L. (2016). Embedding interventions to promote self-determination within multi-tiered systems of supports. *Exceptionality*, *24*(4), 213–224. https://doi.org/10.1080/09362835.2015.1064421

Thurlow, M. L., Ghere, G., Lazarus, S. S., & Liu, K. K. (2020). *MTSS for all: Including students with the most significant cognitive disabilities*. University of Minnesota, National Center on Educational Outcomes/ TIES Center.

10

SDLMI in Community-Based and Virtual Contexts

> When you ask questions, you can learn. When you ask questions, you don't get frustrated. Learning helps to achieve goals!
>
> (Logan Doughty, USA Softball National Office Staff Member and Self-Advocate)

Previous chapters have focused on the importance of self-determination and how the SDLMI can be used to support all students to build self-determination. The primary focus has been using the SDLMI in education contexts, enhancing students' engagement in the general education curriculum (Chapter 7) and in transition planning (Chapter 8) as they set and work toward goals that they identify as meaningful to them. However, the SDLMI and its core components can be used in many ways including with younger students (Shogren et al., 2022), with adults seeking employment (Dean et al., 2017), with anyone setting health and wellness goals (Shogren et al., 2006), or really in any life domain – goals are relevant everywhere! And, increasingly the SDLMI is being used in community settings with groups of adolescents or adults coming together to use the SDLMI to set goals and support each other as they work toward them. This can create more opportunities for people with and without disabilities to come together to build self-determination and support each other as they identify and go after their goals and evaluate and adjust their goals and

DOI: 10.4324/9781003214373-10

the strategies to achieve them. When these activities are led by community members and by people with disabilities, there can be a strong focus on building social and community networks and integrating culturally responsive practices as described in Chapter 6. Community-based implementation can also leverage virtual supports and connections. The need for virtual implementation, in all contexts, increased during the COVID-19 pandemic. What was learned during this time will continue to enhance virtual implementation options and supports, particularly hybrid supports in school and community contexts.

This chapter will highlight ways that the SDLMI has been used in community-based contexts to (1) support adolescents and adults to have more opportunities to work towards goals and (2) build social networks that support them in developing action plans, navigating barriers, and integrating what they have learned into their lives and families and community activities. We will also describe what has been learned about virtual implementation of the SDLMI, including ways the SDLMI can be delivered online in small groups as well as using hybrid delivery models.

Using the SDLMI in Community Contexts: Key Implementation Information

Just as specific materials have been developed to support teachers to use the SDLMI in school and classroom contexts, there are also a set of resources that have been developed to guide how to deliver the SDLMI core components (Student Questions, Teacher Objectives, and Educational Supports) in the community. For example, the SDLMI Community, a set of materials specifically modified for use in community contexts, provides resources including PowerPoints, activities, and technological supports for 14 weekly sessions that target the 12 Student Questions, as well as an introductory session and a closing session that provides an orientation to self-determined actions and reflection and celebration on what is learned, respectively. The SDLMI Community can focus on specific goal buckets, like employment, or can provide a range of goal options, like community engagement, health and wellness, building social networks, depending on the interests and preferences of the group.

The SDLMI Community can also be combined with other interventions. For example, curricula like Finding Me (Ober, 2018) that includes a range of topics (e.g., Where I Live; People I Know and Care About; My Strengths, Interests, and Hobbies; My Dream for My Life) have been implemented prior to the SDLMI Community. This has been particularly useful when working with adults with intellectual and developmental disabilities to build group rapport and identify the funds of knowledge that people with intellectual and developmental disabilities bring to the SDLMI Community (Dean et al., 2022). Groups have also come together to target goals related to employment, community engagement, and health and wellness. Some groups have focused on bringing together people with shared experiences and funds of knowledge; for example the SDLMI Community has been implemented with autistic adolescents, with a specific focus on supporting neurodiversity and incorporating multiple ways for autistic youth to engage and build community and networks as they go after goals that are meaningful to them (Raley et al., 2022). A major focus has also been training people with disabilities to act as co-facilitators in community based SDLMI implementation, providing culturally sustaining implementation of the SDLMI and leveraging lived experiences.

Implementation Schedule and Activities

The SDLMI Community materials are generally organized around weekly or bi-weekly 1-to-1.5-hour meetings organized around the three SDLMI phases (Phase 1: Set a Goal; Phase 2: Take Action; Phase 3: Adjust Goal or Plan). During each session, there is a focus on one SDLMI Student Question, with initial and concluding sessions providing a grounding in self-determination and celebration of what is learned through the sessions. Many community groups also include a concluding presentation, where friends, family, and community members are invited to come and learn about what goals SDLMI group participants set and their plans for the future See Figure 10.1 for a sample implementation schedule for SDLMI Community groups. And, groups or participants in groups can engage in SDLMI Community repeatedly, setting new goals and building more community connections.

The SDLMI Community materials focus on using community-examples. These examples are infused throughout resources for each session including PowerPoints and SDLMI Activity Sheets that reference community examples. SDLMI group members also use Goal Notebooks so they can communicate with supporters outside of SDLMI sessions. For example, SDLMI Community sessions integrate planning for how to support adolescents and adults to share information with their families or their supporters to recruit supports for their SDLMI goals. Figure 10.2 shows samples of pages from the SDLMI Community Goal Notebook, where people can document what they are learning in Phase 1 of the SDLMI and share information with supporters outside of SDLMI Community sessions and build a circle of support for learning about and going after goals. And, all of the support strategies described in previous chapters, including supporting all forms of communication (Chapter 9) and advancing culturally sustaining implementation (Chapter 6) can be integrated into the SDLMI Community.

All SDLMI Community sessions follow a similar structure to enhance group participation and create a routine. Each session

SDLMI Community Implementation Schedule		
Week	Date	Topic
1	Tuesday, February 2	Review SDLMI Terms and Roles; Student Question 1
	Thursday, February 4	Review Student Question 1; Student Question 2
2	Tuesday, February 9	Review Student Question 2; Student Question 3
	Thursday, February 11	Review Student Question 3; Student Question 4
3	Tuesday, February 16	Review Student Question 4; Student Question 5
	Thursday, February 18	Review Student Question 5; Student Question 6
4	Tuesday, February 23	Review Student Question 6; Student Question 7
	Thursday, February 25	Review Student Question 7; Student Question 8
5	Tuesday, March 2	Review Student Question 8; Student Question 9
	Thursday, March 4	Review Student Question 9, Student Question 10
6	Tuesday, March 9	Review Student Question 10; Student Question 11
	Thursday, March 11	Review Student Question 11; Student Question 12
7	Tuesday, March 16	Review Student Question 12; start presentation prep
	Thursday, March 18	Presentation Prep Continued
8	Tuesday, March 23	Presentation Practice
	Thursday, March 25	Presentations

FIGURE 10.1 SDLMI Community Implementation Schedule. Copyright 2022 Kansas University Center on Developmental Disabilities

SDLMI
Self-Determined Learning
Model of Instruction

SDLMI Notebook
Phase 1

For this week, adults continued to work on the Phase 1 of the Self-Determined Learning Model of Instruction (SDLMI).

Phase 1 of the SDLMI: Identify what the goal is

Person Question 3: What must change for me?

- **Think about** improving their abilities **in their goal area**
  Example: working on choosing more fruits and vegetables for healthy snacks
- **Think about** making changes to their environments
  Example: putting a poster of healthy eating on a refrigerator as a reminder

Person Question 4: What can I do to make this happen?

- **Write their own specific, measurable, and observable goal**
  - ○ Measurable: **Something you can count or quantify**
  - ○ Observable: **Something you can see/hear and say whether or not it happened**
  - ○ Specific: **Something clearly identified and defined**

Note. Copyright 2022 Kansas University Center on Developmental Disabilities.

FIGURE 10.2 SDLMI Community Goal Notebooks. Copyright 2022 Kansas University Center on Developmental Disabilities

What Adults Accomplished This Week:

Q. What must change for me?

_____

Q. What can I do to make this happen?

_____

What Supporters Can Do This Week:

• Ask "What do you want to change?"
• Ask "What is your goal?"

What Roles Supporters Play in Promoting Adult Self-Determination:

Supporters provide supports and opportunities for adults to improve their abilities to decide, act, and believe that they can go after their goals.

If you have questions about the SDLMI project, please contact selfdetermination@ku.edu. Please visit self-determination.org for more information about self-determination!

 SELF-DETERMINATION.ORG

FIGURE 10.2 Continued

begins with 5 minutes to chat about people's week as an effort for participants to get to know each other along with a brief mindful breathing exercise and opening mantra co-created by group participants. SDLMI sessions also always review the phase of the SDLMI that participants are engaging in and well as core vocabulary (e.g., short- and long-term goals, goal attainment, problem solving). The majority of the session focuses on the Student Questions, typically beginning with a small group discussion where the co-facilitators engage participants in activities to address the Teacher Objectives, which led to each person answering the Student Question for the day, recording responses in Goal Notebooks using words, pictures, or recording responses. To close, there is a brief review and a summary of what will happen in the next session. All lessons and small group discussions are structured to engage group members in conversation, and there are an array of activities in each session that engage participants in small group work, online activities, and other representations of the content. For example, when defining long-term goals, the SDLMI implementers can provide examples of their long-term goals and ask group members to share theirs.

Goal Buckets

A major focus of the SDLMI Community is supporting a range of goals and building social and community connections to enable those goals. *My SDLMI Story* (Figure 10.3) highlights how Logan Doughty used the SDLMI Community to set an overall goal of finding a reliable way to get to work. His first goal focused on getting his driver's license so he could reliably get to the job he loves every day, working for USA Softball. As Logan describes, while he first focused on getting his driver's license for his SDLMI goal in Phase 1 but then decided to adjust his goal in Phase 3 after he learned more, especially about other supports that could get him to work and aligned with his preferences. As Logan grew in his abilities and skills associated with self-determination (e.g., goal setting, decision making, problem solving) using the SDLMI Community, Logan explored and identified a local transportation he could utilize to reliably get to work and achieve his overall goal of keeping and thriving in the job he loves.

When implementing in the community, a range of goals can be set. Facilitators might focus on one goal bucket like employment or a range of goal buckets. If different goal buckets are targeted, group activities can be organized around different types of goals and brainstorming needed in each domain. SDLMI Community participants have focused on, for example, setting

My name is Logan Doughty. I am 29 years old, and I work for USA Softball. I do lots of stuff at work. Sometimes I work in the gift shop up front or inside with lots of people, and sometimes I work in the stadiums, where I stock up the fridges and water for the athletes. I like to meet athletes! This is the job I've always wanted!

When I think about *self-determination*, I think of when I'm trying to figure something out or dealing with a problem and then being self-determined by self-advocating and saying, "please, come help me." From the SDLMI classes I was in at Oklahoma State University (or OSU), I learned that part of being self-determined is knowing to speak up for myself when I need help or have a problem, or asking questions. Asking questions and finding out the answers helps me to work towards goals. I like to set goals for myself because it is good for me. It helps me to focus on the steps to achieve my goals, and work towards them. Goals are important because they keep me motivated. I want to set more goals at home and at work – that way, I can learn more. When I learn more, I can help people more! I really like it when people help me and I can help them back.

I remember the SDLMI classes at OSU. I talked with a lot of people about what we like to do, and what we want to do in the future. I wanted to learn to drive, so I set a goal to get my driver's license. I thought about it and knew that is what I wanted to do. I learned about the ways to achieve my goal, and what steps it would take. I learned to ask questions and ask people around me for help when I needed it. They helped me create an action plan and helped me learn more about my goals. Later, I decided not to get my driver's license because I was afraid of wrecking since there are a lot of cars around. So, I changed my goal to learning to use SendARide, a transportation service in Oklahoma City. Now, I take SendARide to work every day.

My advice for people working on being self-determined is to always ask questions. When you ask questions, you can learn. When you ask questions, you don't get frustrated. Learning helps to achieve goals!

I think working on being self-determined using the SDLMI is really great.

—Logan Doughty, USA Softball National Office Staff Member and Self-Advocate

FIGURE 10.3 My SDLMI Story: Using the SDLMI to Work Towards Goals that Are Important in My Life. Copyright 2022 Kansas University Center on Developmental Disabilities

goals related to employment (e.g., "I want to work at a veterinarian," "I want to get a new job") or health (e.g., "I want to exercise more," "I want to be able to walk around the park"). And, community-based implementation has been just as impactful as school-based implementation, particularly in supporting participants to break down and develop action plans. As one adult said, it allowed them to "figure out a little bit about how maybe to set the goals and maybe now try more." Another said, they are "trying to do it in smaller steps than you know just all at once or whatever" (Dean et al., 2022).

When considering SDLMI implementation in the community, it is important to think about key challenges that can emerge. We mentioned how important it is to support communication with families, teachers, and other supporters. If the person is learning and setting goals in their SDLMI Community group, they will need a range of supports to take action toward those goals at home and in the community. For example, if a person is setting goals related to employment their goals need to be communicated to and supported by other systems and people that are providing employment supports, using tools like Figure 10.2. This can also be a time when SDLMI Community group members and facilitators work together to identify systemic barriers and advocacy that they may undertake individually or as a group. For example, there are significant barriers to accessing competitive, integrated employment and accessing ongoing education. SDLMI Community groups can discuss these issues as they are learning about barriers and advocacy. Transportation can also be an important consideration as people have to be able to get to groups in the community. Making sure groups are near an accessible transportation location is important as is planning carefully to ensure equity in access and participation. Considering virtual and hybrid options can be useful to promote access, particularly in rural communities, as we'll discuss in the next section.

Using the SDLMI in Virtual Contexts: Key Implementation Information

The SDLMI Community can be implemented virtually, or can incorporate virtual elements using a hybrid delivery model. For example, the SDLMI Community has been implemented during one-on-one and small group virtual sessions on videoconferencing platforms (e.g., Zoom). During the COVID-19 pandemic, all SDLMI instruction in the community or in school contexts was implemented virtually, providing important insight that can guide the ongoing use of virtual and hybrid options. Delivering the SDLMI virtually, like any instruction, takes careful planning to ensure that there are engagement strategies the make the SDLMI core components relevant and meaningful for all participants.

When implementing the SDLMI virtually, the same general structure can be used (i.e., each session is focused on one of the 12 SDLMI Student Questions as well as introduction and celebration sessions); however, online engagement tools can also enhance instruction and participation. For example, several videoconferencing platforms allow for the use of breakout rooms in addition to whole-group meeting spaces, enabling students or community groups to see each other in a large group but also have smaller group and one-to-one connection opportunities to talk through their SDLMI goals, action plans, and self-evaluation strategies. These small group opportunities facilitated by breakout rooms supports the development of a circle of supporters as youth and adults set and work toward goals.

As trained SDLMI implementers engage youth and young adults in virtual implementation of the SDLMI, several engagement tools can be helpful like asking students to use videoconference platform features like emojis or using the chat box to provide positive reinforcement when their peer shares a success they have experienced as they use the SDLMI (e.g., trying a new self-management strategy to take five deep breaths before a test and learning that this worked for them). SDLMI implementers engaging students in the SDLMI virtually can also use other engagement tools and activities like creating their own games, like collaboratively working together to identify a five-letter word the facilitator has picked ahead of time and aligns with the session's content (e.g., "goals" or "track").

Implementing the SDLMI virtually provides another tool to engage people in learning about self-determination using best practices in virtual instruction and supporting all people to learn and grow in their self-determination. Virtual delivery options as well as using virtual activities and resources to promote engagement during in-person activities provides another way to make the SDLMI meaningful and accessible to even greater numbers of students and adults with and without disabilities.

References

Dean, E. E., Burke, K. M., Shogren, K. A., & Wehmeyer, M. L. (2017). Promoting self-determination and integrated employment through the self-determined career development model. *Advances in Neurodevelopmental Disorders*, *1*, 55–62. https://doi.org/10.1007/s41252-017-0011-y

Dean, E. E., Hagiwara, M., Jones, J., Gallus, K., & Shogren, K. A. (2022). Promoting self-determination in community contexts: Experiences with implementing the Self-Determined Learning Model of Instruction. *Inclusion*, *10*(1), 53–70. https://doi.org/10.1352/2326-6988-10.1.53

Ober, J. (2018). *Finding Me: How to advocate for the life you want.* The Ohio State University Nisonger Center.

Raley, S. K., Edwards, B., Bumble, J. L., Shogren, K. A., & Henley, R. C. (2022). Enhancing self-determination for autistic youth and young adults using the Self-Determined Learning Model of Instruction [Manuscript in preparation].

Shogren, K. A., Wehmeyer, M. L., Reese, R. M., & O'Hara, D. (2006). Promoting self-determination in health and medical care: A critical component of addressing health disparities in people with intellectual disabilities. *Journal of Policy and Practice in Intellectual Disabilities*, *3*(2), 105–113. https://doi.org/10.1111/j.1741-1130.2006.00061.x

Shogren, K. A., Zimmerman, K. N., & Toste, J. R. (2022). The potential for developing and supporting self-determination in early childhood and elementary classrooms. In J. McLeskey, F. Spooner, B. Algozzine, & N. L. Waldron (Eds.), *Handbook of effective inclusive elementary schools: Research and practice* (2nd ed.). Routledge.

11

Future Directions in SDLMI Practice

People with disabilities pushed for self-determination. True to its start, people with disabilities can and should lead work to promote self-determination, like using the SDLMI, so their needs are met.

(Brad Linnenkamp, Self-Advocate, Community Liaison, and Researcher, Kansas University Center on Developmental Disabilities)

This book highlighted the importance and impact of self-determination in the lives of *all* students, with a particular focus on transition-age students with disabilities. We hope the chapters provided relevant information on how to use the evidence-based Self-Determined Learning Model of Instruction (SDLMI) to promote self-determination in school and community contexts. The SDLMI can be used to empower all students to be causal agents in their lives as they set and work toward goals they identify as meaningful and advocate for themselves and their communities. We encourage you to think about the ways that you can use the SDLMI and support students to build self-determination in your settings, but also how *you can be an advocate and a change agent*, bringing evidence-based practices designed to enhance self-determination, like the SDLMI, to your schools and communities. Think about how powerful it could be if you are supporting students with disabilities in small groups to set goals

DOI: 10.4324/9781003214373-11

in transition planning and, at the same time, those students are learning to set goals in their academic, general education classes with their peers. This would highlight to everyone in your setting that building self-determination is for *everyone* and opportunities to set and work toward goals across environments is key!

The chapters in this book highlight the many ways that the SDLMI can be used (e.g., in inclusive contexts—Chapter 7; in transition planning—Chapter 8; and in the community and virtual contexts—Chapter 10). We also highlight the range of ways the SDLMI can be embedded into a tiered approach (Chapter 5) with support and planning from school leaders. Chapter 6 highlights how we can strive to make the SDLMI and self-determination instruction culturally responsive and aligned with students' funds of knowledge to become, as Banks et al. (2022) describes, "agents of their own life experiences" developing "cultural agency" and "constructing positive cultural identities" (p. 98). We further elaborate on how students that communicate in diverse ways can be supported as they use the SDLMI (Chapter 9), enabling inclusion and recognition of various communication styles, preferences, and needs. We also suggest ways that assessment information can be used to empower students, families, and communities to advance equity and inclusion in self-determination instruction (Chapter 4).

Even with all this information and the substantial progress made since leaders in the disability field pushed for a greater emphasis on self-determination, as you read about in Chapter 1, there remains work to be done to advance equity not only in self-determination outcomes, but also in how we provide self-determination instruction and supports. In particular, there is a need to further explore how to embed self-determination instruction in practice and better understand the most effective supports for implementing the SDLMI in ways that address the needs of all students, families, teachers, and community members. Throughout this book, we have described what we have learned through research and practice over the past two decades. What we have learned and the resulting strategies described in this book can be used to create opportunities for students, families, educators, and other community members to work in partnership to advance self-determination, challenging structural barriers to self-determination and valued postschool outcomes (e.g., competitive integrated employment, community participation). We hope that the next two decades brings even more growth and development in self-determination practice and further advances a focus on equity and inclusion in self-determination research.

In this final book chapter, we highlight areas that we see as critical in shaping the future of self-determination practice, including ways that we hope the SDLMI will be used in the future by students, families, teachers, and other community members to support goals identified as meaningful in their lives and valued postschool outcomes. However, these are only our thoughts at this moment, and we look forward to practitioners, like you, as well as students, families, and community members informing and leading new directions that push research and practice further than we have imagined. Creating change takes partnerships, so we hope you and others inspired by this book will build community around the common goal of supporting all transition-age students, inclusive of students with disabilities, to become self-determined. We particularly invite ongoing efforts to ensure that young people who experience marginalization in our society are empowered to critique and provide direction for future advancement. We organize our thoughts, to be expanded on by others, into four areas below.

People with Disabilities as SDLMI Implementers, Educators, Peer Supports, and Leaders

This chapter started with a quote from Brad Linnenkamp, a person with intellectual and developmental disabilities, who has forged a career path aligned with his interests and desire to advance equity in the disability field. As further described in Brad's Self-Determination Story in Figure 11.1, Brad's focus across all of his roles (e.g., researcher, leader, peer support) has been on creating opportunities for the involvement and leadership of people with disabilities in all aspects of their lives. For Brad, this includes pushing the disability research and practice

I have played multiple roles in the disability field, including as a self-advocate fighting for my rights and the rights of other people with intellectual and developmental disabilities (IDD). I will always be an advocate no matter what my job is. But, now I have transitioned from being a paid self-advocate at the Self Advocate Coalition of Kansas to being a paid researcher and community liaison at the Kansas University Center on Developmental Disabilities (KUCDD). In my role at KUCDD, I make sure the voices of people with IDD actually influence research and how that research is used in practice. At KUCDD, we do a lot of research focused on self-determination and using the SDLMI. I lead work to make sure the SDLMI is relevant to people with disabilities and that people can use evidence-based interventions, like the SDLMI, to help their community and break down barriers. Unfortunately, not all researchers and practitioners recognize how I and others with disabilities can contribute, although it is getting better. In fact, over my life, lots of people have assumed that I—because of my disability—could not do research or implement interventions like the SDLMI. But, it is important for me to bring my life experiences to the research in a way that only I can. I also want the voices of other disabled advocates included in the research. It challenges me, but also provides me with a source of pride and impacts others with disabilities and my community and, I think, teachers and other professionals.

It's important to say that there are challenges to implementing interventions and leading research. Oftentimes processing the information that is presented in trainings and in meetings is difficult, and I need to ask people to explain things in a way that makes sense. At first, this was difficult, but then I realized that other people benefitted from making sure discussions were clear and structured and questions and expectations were directly stated. These experiences led me to push forward the work we do at KUCDD focused on creating plain language trainings and materials to support everyone, including people with disabilities, to be SDLMI facilitators, peer supports, and leaders.

My key message is—people need to stop assuming things about people with disabilities. We can be SDLMI trainers, facilitators, teachers, researchers, leaders, or whatever roles we can imagine. Too often in the past people have put words in my mouth or made assumptions before they got to know me. But, I can speak for myself and I can teach and support other people with disabilities to speak for themselves and be self-determined. I understand the barriers and needs of people with disabilities because I have encountered many of them too. And, I want all of us to be sure people with disabilities are leading and co-leading research about people with disabilities.

I think we can do this together, as a community, recognizing all of our contributions.

—Brad Linnenkamp, Self-Advocate, Community Liaison, and Researcher,
Kansas University Center on Developmental Disabilities

FIGURE 11.1 My SDLMI Story: People with Disabilities as SDLMI Implementers, Peer Supports, and Leaders. Copyright 2022 Kansas University Center on Developmental Disabilities

field to engage in more participatory, collaborative, and inclusive implementation of the SDLMI that is led and co-led by people that experience disability. Brad shows the power of this way of thinking. Who better to support people with disabilities in navigating barriers as they set and work towards goals than a person who deeply understands those barriers and can share how they identified solutions in their own life? Ricky Broussard shared a similar perspective in Chapter 6 when he described how he acted as a peer support, delivering self-determination instruction to young people with disabilities. The power of shared experiences and role models who share cultural identities cannot be overstated to advance cultural agency and self-determination. We hope that inclusive and participatory approaches to research and practice will continue to grow with a recognition that people with disabilities, inclusive of people with disabilities who experience other forms of marginalization, can and do make significant and positive impacts as educators, peer supports, and leaders in implementation of the SDLMI and self-determination research, policy, and practice. We hope that schools and communities will increasingly embrace models that advance participation and career pathways that enable people with disabilities to share their funds of knowledge and expertise, including by implementing and leading the SDLMI.

Scaling Up Supports and Implementation

We have highlighted throughout this book the various supports for training, implementation, and tracking outcomes that are available through the SDLMI and its associated training materials and resources. However, there is a critical need to determine the most effective ways to embed self-determination instruction throughout the life course, in multi-tiered systems of support (Chapter 5), providing educators the supports they need (e.g., coaching, online materials for intervention delivery and tracking of outcomes). Only by using best practices in coaching and promoting the adoption of self-determination interventions by schools, districts, and state departments of education can sustained and long-term supports for infusing self-determination throughout all instructional activities take place. We hope that an ongoing focus on the most effective (including cost effective) ways to deliver self-determination instruction will support an understanding of the key ingredients needed for scaling-up use of the SDLMI. For example, determining how to embed research-based coaching and training practices into schools' planning and priorities are needed, as are alternative and supplemental ways to deliver self-determination instruction. For example, the Goal Setting Challenge App (GSC App) is being developed to deliver the SDLMI via technology (Mazzotti et al., 2022), with positive impacts on students' goal attainment and reduced demands on teacher time for instructional planning (Shogren et al., 2022). Ongoing development is needed to leverage what we are learning about technology and technological supports for learning.

Home–School–Community Connections

As we have noted throughout this book, and as is well known to all educators, building strong connections across home, school, and the community are essential to educational outcomes. Families can and should play an active role in supporting students to achieve their vision for life beyond high school as they are often viewed as the "linchpin" in the transition to adulthood. Families simultaneously support navigating the transition from school-based services and supports to the adult service-delivery system, continuing to provide support, and advocating for appropriate services. Despite research documenting the benefits of family engagement, families experience many barriers to meaningful involvement in school-based interventions (Boehm et al., 2015). These barriers include a lack of family-school communication, an absence of training for practitioners to meaningfully engage families, and exacerbated and unique barriers for families from culturally and linguistically marginalized backgrounds. While self-determination instruction and the SDLMI have long highlighted the importance of engaging families and communities in SDLMI implementation, there is a need for a re-prioritization of building connections across home–school–community and promoting cultural sustainability. There is an opportunity to further explore how to promote communication about goals and future planning in school-based interventions and to infuse the voices, experiences, and funds of knowledge of families and communities into the academic curriculum, as well as Individualized Education Program (IEP) and transition goal development for students with disabilities.

Centering Multiple Marginalized Experiences to Elevate All

Finally, as has been mentioned throughout this book and particularly in Chapter 6, there is a need to advance efforts to engage in culturally sustainable implementation of the SDLMI. This must be infused across all efforts to advance self-determination and while we present this as a separate chapter in this text, we want to emphasize that the centrality of rooting self-determination and SDLMI instruction in efforts to advance equity and leverage the funds of knowledge of all community members, particularly those who have been marginalized or multiply marginalized in existing research and practice. As highlighted in Chapter 3, research on the SDLMI has not yet adequately addressed issues of racial and disability justice and their intersection in all aspects of implementation. This must change. Advancing equity necessitates identifying and dismantling systemic barriers to the representation and inclusion of the identities and funds of knowledge of marginalized people with disabilities, people of color with disabilities, and other historically marginalized communities. To advance inclusion, and inclusion in self-determination research and practice, we must welcome, represent, and value the identities, ways of learning, and approaches to determining one's goals and pathways. Advancing inclusion and cultural justice necessitates action, intention, and regular practice from all of us. It requires a focus on elevating the voices and challenging the systemic barriers faced by people that experience multiple forms of marginalization. Our final message to you is: *Be an advocate and change agent* who works to center multiply marginalized experiences in self-determination research and practice, elevating these experiences and voices to advance "Nothing About Us Without Us."

References

Banks, J., Smith, P., & Charington Neal, D. (2022). Identity politics: Exploring disCrit's potential to empower activities and collective resistance. In S. A. Annamma, B. Ferri, & D. Connor (Eds.), *DisCrit expanded: Reverberations, ruptures, and inquiries* (pp. 96–111). Teachers College Press.

Boehm, T. L., Carter, E. W., & Taylor, J. L. (2015). Family quality of life during the transition to adulthood for individuals with intellectual disability and/or autism spectrum disorders. *American Journal on Intellectual and Developmental Disabilities*, *120*(5), 395–411. https://doi.org/10.1352/1944-7558-120.5.395

Mazzotti, V. L., Shogren, K. A., Stewart-Ginsburg, J. H., Wysenski, D., Burke, K. M., & Hildebrandt, L. (2022). Development of the goal-setting challenge app: Engaging users to promote self-determination. *International Journal of Disability, Development, and Education*, *69*(1), 331–351. https://doi.org/10.1080/1034912X.2021.1959022

Shogren, K. A., Mazzotti, V. L., Hicks, T. A., Raley, S. K., Gerasimova, D., Pace, J. R., Kwiatek, S. M., Fredrick, D., Stewart-Ginsburg, J. H., Chapman, R. A., & Wysenski, D. (2022). The goal setting challenge app: Impact on transition goal attainment outcomes of students with disabilities [Manuscript submitted for publication].

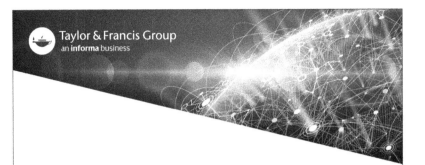